THE LAYMAN'S BIBLE COMMENTARY

THE LAYMAN'S BIBLE COMMENTARY
IN TWENTY-FIVE VOLUMES

THE LAYMAN'S BIBLE COMMENTARY

Balmer H. Kelly, *Editor*

Donald G. Miller *Associate Editors* Arnold B. Rhodes

Dwight M. Chalmers, *Editor, John Knox Press*

VOLUME 1

INTRODUCTION TO THE BIBLE

Kenneth J. Foreman

Balmer H. Kelly

Arnold B. Rhodes

Bruce M. Metzger

Donald G. Miller

JOHN KNOX PRESS

Atlanta

10 9 8 7 6 5 4 3 2

Complete set: ISBN: 0-8042-3086-2
This volume: 0-8042-3061-7
Library of Congress Card Number: 59-10454
First paperback edition 1982
Printed in the United States of America
John Knox Press
Atlanta, Georgia 30365

PREFACE

The LAYMAN'S BIBLE COMMENTARY is based on the conviction that the Bible has the Word of good news for the whole world. The Bible is not the property of a special group. It is not even the property and concern of the Church alone. It is given to the Church for its own life but also to bring God's offer of life to all mankind—wherever there are ears to hear and hearts to respond.

It is this point of view which binds the separate parts of the LAYMAN'S BIBLE COMMENTARY into a unity. There are many volumes and many writers, coming from varied backgrounds, as is the case with the Bible itself. But also as with the Bible there is a unity of purpose and of faith. The purpose is to clarify the situations and language of the Bible that it may be more and more fully understood. The faith is that in the Bible there is essentially one Word, one message of salvation, one gospel.

The LAYMAN'S BIBLE COMMENTARY is designed to be a concise non-technical guide for the layman in personal study of his own Bible. Therefore, no biblical text is printed along with the comment upon it. This commentary will have done its work precisely to the degree in which it moves its readers to take up the Bible for themselves.

The writers have used the Revised Standard Version of the Bible as their basic text. Occasionally they have differed from this translation. Where this is the case they have given their reasons. In the main, no attempt has been made either to justify the wording of the Revised Standard Version or to compare it with other translations.

The objective in this commentary is to provide the most helpful explanation of fundamental matters in simple, up-to-date terms. Exhaustive treatment of subjects has not been undertaken.

In our age knowledge of the Bible is perilously low. At the same time there are signs that many people are longing for help in getting such knowledge. Knowledge of and about the Bible is, of course, not enough. The grace of God and the work of the Holy Spirit are essential to the renewal of life through the Scriptures. It is in the happy confidence that the great hunger for the Word is a sign of God's grace already operating within men, and that the Spirit works most wonderfully where the Word is familiarly known, that this commentary has been written and published.

THE EDITORS AND
THE PUBLISHERS

INTRODUCTION TO THE BIBLE

What Is the Bible?
Kenneth J. Foreman

The History of the People of God
Balmer H. Kelly

The Message of the Bible
Arnold B. Rhodes

How We Got the Bible
Bruce M. Metzger

How to Study the Bible
Donald G. Miller

WHAT IS THE BIBLE?

The Bible is a book not always easy to understand. Otherwise, why read commentaries? Its most important truths can be understood without benefit of commentary, but the difficulties are there.

Some of the difficulties come from the form of the Bible. When we ask, What *is* the Bible? we can answer the question on various levels. Let us begin with what is most simple, plain, and undeniable. The Bible is, in fact, *ancient oriental literature*.

Consider each of those words in turn, to see what they mean as clues to interpreting the Bible.

The Form of the Bible

First, *the Bible is ancient*. It was not all written at the same time. The earliest sections of the Old Testament were written perhaps as far back as twelve centuries before Christ, and the latest sections of it within two hundred years of Christ's birth. That is a span of one thousand years. The New Testament was done, comparatively speaking, in a hurry, the earliest and the latest writings in it being no more than a century apart, if so much. The content of the entire Bible as we have it has been in existence for roughly eighteen centuries.

The great age of the Bible is important to remember, when we come to think about the Bible's meaning. It does make two difficulties for the modern reader. First is the *language*. Hebrew, in which almost the entire Old Testament was written, was never widely spoken, seldom the tongue of a dominant race or nation. On the contrary, Greek, the language of the New Testament, at the time of Christ was the universal language of the most civilized part of Europe, indeed of the whole Mediterranean world, from Jordan to Gibraltar. Today, however, Hebrew is known by comparatively few persons, and Greek has not only changed greatly but has also become a minority language, like Danish or Korean or Tamil. Consequently, to reach most modern readers *the Bible has to be translated*. Parts of it have been translated into more than 1000 different dialects and languages.

The attempt to translate an ancient language into a modern one always runs into troubles, for no language can ever bring out *precisely* what is said in another, though the general meaning may be quite clear. Consequently also, "the" Bible is never the Latin, English, German, or any other translation. *The* Bible is always the original Hebrew and Greek. To be sure, the original Hebrew and Greek writings have been lost; not a single page is known to exist as it came from the writer's or editor's hand. What we have are the oldest available copies of the now lost originals.

We can be reassured, however, by this fact, on which all experts agree: In our present English translation we do have a very good translation of Hebrew and Greek manuscripts which are certainly very like the actual "autographs," that is to say, the writings as they left the authors' desks. Nevertheless, what we have is always a translation, not the "very words" Paul or anyone else used.

The other difficulty is not the language but the *thought*. People in bygone centuries lived in a different world from ours. They did not understand the world they lived in; they could not control it, as we do our world. Our twentieth-century world is vastly different even from the sixteenth-century world, but even more different from the world of the ancient past. This also raises problems for the Bible reader. If it is sometimes hard to figure out why Grandpa thinks as he does, when he is no more than half a century older than you, it is much harder to figure out why someone of a different race and of a civilization twenty centuries or more before your time thought as he did. It is true, nevertheless, that human nature is always basically much the same, in spite of all changes. The modern reader finds that even with all the difficulties he does feel drawn to a real sympathy with these characters who lived, suffered, believed, and died so long, long ago.

Second, *the Bible is oriental*. Not Chinese-style oriental, not even Indian-style, not quite Persian. More like the Middle East than any part of the world we now know. Most of the people described in it, or writing any part of it, lived "east of Suez." We make a great mistake if we fancy them as modern Americans or Europeans.

For one thing, they did not have the passion for precision that we have, or like to think that we have. Some readers of the Bible find a contradiction in the statement that the circumference of the great reservoir, called a "sea," in the Temple of Solomon was three times its diameter (I Kings 7:23). It couldn't have been, of course; every schoolboy knows that it could only have been 3.1416 times, not 3. But no ancient writer, and no oriental writer or reader, would have cared about decimals. In the world where the Bible was written, people did not care about exact figures as a modern educated person does.

Another thing is the matter of quotations. Nowadays we have laws of copyright, and nearly every book carries a warning not to quote any part of it without permission. In the ancient oriental world an author felt free to quote anyone at any time without permission, and without giving his references as a modern writer must when quoting. So you will find many writers of the Bible using material they got from other Bible writers, or from other places, without mentioning their sources.

A third oriental touch is the fondness of the Middle Easterner for figurative, picturesque language. These were not Anglo-Saxon or German prose-minded people, they were poetic by nature. Imagination was the very spirit of their thinking. So a modern reader who lacks entirely the quality of imagination, who always thinks literally or as a scientist would, misses the spirit of much that the Bible writers put quite naturally into poetic, figurative, colorful speech.

Then, too, *the Bible is literature,* that is to say, writings. This does not mean that all parts of it have a high literary value, or that just any paragraph in it will be a literary gem. Parts of the Bible do rate high for sheer literary charm and power, and professors of literature from Harvard to Heidelberg will praise it accordingly. But however highly polished many parts of the Bible are, no Bible writer put polish ahead of truth. Getting the message across was the first thing; literary style came a poor second.

Nevertheless, this is literature, of an amazing variety, some prose, some poetry. It comes to us, in English Protestant Bibles, in sixty-six "books," some of them not a page long, and the longest under one hundred pages. These are divided into the well-known Old and New Testaments, with thirty-nine and twenty-seven books respectively. Most of us learned the arrangement in Sunday school: in the Old Testament, Law, History, Poetry, Prophecy; in the New Testament, Gospels, Acts, Letters, Revelation.

The list does not begin to give an idea of the variety of this literature. The so-called books of the Law are mostly not law at all, but stories, at first of individuals, later of the desert clans calling themselves the "children of Israel." The historical books (which the Jews themselves did not call historical, but "former prophets") give us episodes or incidents in Israel over a period of centuries.

The next division is called "poetic," but riffling through the pages of your Revised Standard Version will convince you that there is almost as much poetry in the prophets as there is in the "poetic" books. There is really no one word that describes these five books in the middle of the Old Testament. One of these is a drama, Job; one is the great collection of five ancient hymnbooks, known as the Psalms; one a collection of sayings, wise and witty, the Proverbs; one a series of short essays in a dark mood, Ecclesiastes; and finally a bouquet of love poetry, the Song of Solomon. Following this there is a collection of prophecies, so disarranged that today's reader, without a guide, finds it the most puzzling part of the Bible.

The New Testament begins with the story of Jesus, told four times over. Then comes the story of the beginnings of the Christian Church and the part that was, in the main, actually written first—the letters of Paul. The Church, as it slowly sifted out of early Christian writings what we call the New Testament, included some few writings of other Christian leaders besides Paul and the authors of the Gospels; and at the end put the strange book called Revelation, not written last but surely belonging there, as it looks forward to the final future of man.

In this great and unique collection of writings, by many men— stories, dramas, chronicles, legends, poems of nature and love and war, hymns for public and private worship, letters, sermons, biographies, essays—not the least remarkable feature is that a unity of meaning and message can be seen through the vast variety of forms of expression. What the meaning and message are, can best be discovered by reading it. To help readers understand it is the aim of this whole commentary and all the commentaries ever written. For a fuller discussion, see the article, "The Message of the Bible." Meanwhile, consider how the Bible is held together by what may be called its plot. It is an immense thing. The stage is gigantic, the time scheme is enormous, the action takes in the entire human race, the whole world. We even have glimpses of worlds beyond this one. It is the story of the vast conflict between good and evil, portrayed as a conflict between God and the

Devil. It is only in the very last chapters that the end is glimpsed, when Satan is finally overthrown and the triumph of God is complete; when man is won at last to God; when God wipes away every tear and dwells with men in the new heavens and the new earth.

Christianity is a book religion. This is nothing against it. No bookless religion ever got far. Of the world's living religions which have as many as a million adherents, every one is a book religion. If the reader has ever wondered whether all religions are saying the same thing, or has ever supposed that one religion's Bible is as good as another, he should compare the Bible with any other book held to be sacred. He will not need any persuasion to see that the Bible is not only in a class by itself: a light comes from it that comes from no other book.

The Meaning of the Bible

The meaning of anything is more important than its form; this is true of the Bible as it is of all other things. We can get at the meaning of the Bible by asking the simple question: *Why has it been preserved?* Why have so much patience, stubborn devotion, even martyrdom, gone into the preservation and handing on of *this* literature? Other books decay and are forgotten, but not this one.

The Bible has been cherished and preserved, for one thing, because *it is intensely human.* If one turns to the Bible for a blueprint of heaven he will never find it. What he will find is an account of matters here on this planet. In the very opening verses, after that all-inclusive "God created the heavens and the earth," the next sentence begins: "The earth . . ." This green earth is the scene of the long story. The war between God and evil may cover the universe, so far as we know; but the battles described in Scripture are on our small earth.

The Bible is human, because it comes from experience and appeals to experience; not just any experience, trivial or meaningless, but the most universal and profound experiences known to the human race. And of course, the most profound moments of human existence are those in which the spirit of man becomes alive to the presence of God.

This is the other reason why the Bible has been passionately preserved through the centuries: *in it and through it men have perceived the voice and learned the will of God.* It is true that the Bible is interested in the human adventure; it is true that we can learn more about human nature from reading the Bible than from living in New York. But this alone is not why men have cherished this ancient library. The most prominent character in the Bible, after all, is God himself. John Calvin said that the things man *must* know are only two: God, and himself. It is these two that come clearly before us in the Christian Bible, and not as two separate things. Rather, the Bible's whole concern is with the relations between God and man, or for each reader, the relation between God and me.

The Viewpoint of Faith

Up to this point nothing has been said about the Bible which could not be agreed to by everybody, from saint to atheist. The Bible *is* literature of the kind described. People who hold by it do so because they see themselves in it and because they find that God has something to say to them in it, something which they "cannot choose but hear." But at this point we come to the difference between the viewpoint of faith and the viewpoint of unbelief. Everybody agrees that people have found these values in the Bible. Millions of people have taken the Bible to be a revelation of both man and God. But the question is, *is* the Bible such a revelation? Does the Bible really tell us the truth? Is God here speaking? Or is the whole story of men's attachment to the Scriptures just part of the "history of an illusion"? Men *see* great things here. *Are* they here?

At this point and from this point we set ourselves on the side of faith. The Bible itself can be called a confession of faith on the part of its many writers. They were not trying to build a theology. Many writers of the Bible were not "theological" in the technical sense. But all the Bible writers, in one way or another, to one degree or another, say their say under the influence of their un-hesitating faith in the same living God. They never try to prove that God exists, they take it for granted. All readers of the Bible can see this much.

But the skeptic only shakes his head and thinks, "What fools these mortals be!" while the man of faith, the man with an "ear to hear," finds himself *sharing the faith of the Bible writers themselves.* It could almost be said that the man of faith reads the Bible from *inside* the Bible. He is like a man who has stepped into a cathedral and, looking up, sees around him in the windows a magnificence, a beauty, which the man on the outside sees only as dim patterns in dusty, dark window frames. The non-believer can only say: The Bible is thought by many to be the Word of God. The believer says: I am one of those who think that the Bible is the Word of God. And *I am certain* that I not only *think* this is true; it *is* true.

What comes to me from the Bible (the believer goes on) comes, so to speak, as though through those telephone cables which can carry many messages at the same time. I hear voices from the past, but also a message for today, every today. I hear the voices of long-dead men, but also in their voices I hear the voice of the living God. I read stories of what has happened on this earth, green with meadow and forest, or red with blood of battles; yet in these happenings I see a purpose, God's purpose, working out from generation to generation. In the Bible are words of men—what men thought, felt, believed, hoped; but in, beyond, and above these words of men, I hear the Word of God.

Some Problems

This does not mean that we have dodged all the problems, much less that we have solved them. The very facts at which we have been looking, the very faith which we share, raise questions we must face. If not all Christians give the same answer to these questions, that should not disturb us. There will always be different answers. There can be no final, infallible, and guaranteed answer—unless one can believe that some church or some church officer is infallible. But the questions are here, and they call for some sensible, reasonable, more-than-likely answers. Books have been written on each of these. What follows here is no more than an introduction to some of them.

The Bible as History

Some problems grow out of the fact that the Bible is a human book, written by men in particular situations, each with his own outlook, education, limitations, and so on.

The first of these problems comes from the fact that much of the Bible is made up of stories. These may be short anecdotes or they may be accounts of the birth, life, and death of a nation.

The "history" may say something about the time before there was any universe at all (if that can be called time); or at the other end it may say something about the "time" when the universe shall have ceased to exist; but it is chiefly about events as they were experienced by the writers, or by people whose experiences had come down to the writers by word-of-mouth tradition or by earlier writings.

At first glance this would seem to raise no problem. There is nothing mysterious about history! But when you start reading the Bible carefully, you find that this is not like any history you ever read in school or since. For one thing, this is not "objective," take-it-or-leave-it history-writing, like a news column in a paper. It is frankly viewpointed, slanted, "subjective" history. The writers do not hesitate to call some men and events bad, and others good. The writers are not simple reporters, they are praisers and blamers.

For another thing, this is most extraordinary history because of its central character: God. He is the subject of the first sentence; he appears in the closing sentence. He appears all the way through. He is not Something that people think about, argue over, or pray to—though he is that, to be sure. He is *the God who acts*. He does all the most important things. No "scientific" historian would undertake to mention God in his pages in this way. God would appear, if at all, only in some description of a religion. But here in the Bible, God is vividly present all the time. The stories do not speak of God as if he only occasionally reached his hand into the affairs of men, as one might set the hands of a watch that can run pretty well by itself. God is more like the mainspring of the watch, except that in the Bible he is never a blind force like a spring or a storm. He is always a Person who has personal friends and enemies, and acts in personal ways.

Now the problem is: Is this really history? As "pure" history—meaning just what you could catch on a moving picture film with sound track—of course the Bible does not qualify. For "good" and "evil" are judgments of fact, not the facts themselves. They can be right judgments or wrong judgments, but no camera and no tape recorder can by itself record "bad" or "good." Bible history, then, is something more than history; it is "history-as-interpreted," not bare events but events as they are judged, valued, praised, or condemned. To put this in another way, what we have in the historical parts of the Bible is not history after all, but a religious philosophy of history—events and circumstances seen through the eyes of a believer in God.

The history of the Bible is not a simple chronicle of events. It is an extended interpretation of selected events along one line, namely, the *purpose of God.* (For a discussion of the line the Bible follows, see the articles on the message of the Bible, and on the history of the people of God.)

When we ask the natural question, Is the interpretation the Bible gives to events a true one? we come to the important question of *revelation,* of which more later. At present we must note what is meant by the often quoted saying that the Bible was written from faith, to faith. To say that it was written from or out of faith is to say that its writers believed that God was working through the events they describe. To say that it is written to faith is to say that the Bible can be fully appreciated only by those who share the faith of the writers, and who agree that these religious interpretations of history are *right.*

The Bible as Experience

Another problem arising from the nature of the Bible as literature concerns experience. All literature begins from the experience of human beings—and this experience may include thoughts they think as well as events that happen to them. Literature speaks to those who have had similar experiences. It awakens further experiences, perhaps far in the future. This is true not only of what an English teacher would recognize as literature. It is true of any writing which readers find interesting, such as detective stories, accounts of scientific expeditions, or the descriptions of surgical operations in medical journals. Even comic books have their effects on children. But always it is the same pattern: (1) Somebody has an experience. (2) He, or someone else, writes about it. (3) Another person, or millions of other persons, by reading about it, think, "That's for me."

But here is the problem, not only about the Bible but about any literature, including plays, movies, and so forth: *Is* this really for me? Would I be doing right to have the same experience? Does this story, this poem, or this play on television lead me or mislead me? We can put the question formally in these words: Just how *normative* is the experience described? De Quincey wrote *Confessions of an Opium Eater.* Should I also become a drug addict? A script writer turns out a screenplay which is advertised as a love story but is actually glamorized adultery. Shall I commit the same sin because a movie producer makes me think the best people do it? Another author writes most persuasively out of his own deep pessimism that life is meaningless. Shall I become a follower of such modern apostles of despair? Literature comes out of experience, yes; but some of it is good experience, to be imitated and shared if possible, while some of it is bad, to be feared and avoided if possible.

To come back to the question: How normative are the experiences which the Bible sets forth? How true are the points of view of the biblical characters? How far should I follow the examples set here? "Noah got drunk—why shouldn't I?" was the question of a backwoods alcoholic. If the Bible, a book written by men, expresses the life and thought of men, how shall I be sure it does not mislead me?

To this question the Christian reader has two answers. The answers do not clear up everything; they leave much to be thought over and discussed. But they cover the main points. One answer is to say: The experiences here described are true and genuine. *This is the way men are.* The brutality, the crookedness, the filth and hypocrisy, are all here; there is no denying it. It is stupid to shut one's eyes to it and claim, for example, that Abraham and David and Paul were sinless men. But even the ugly facts are valuable to us, because this is really a candid camera. We see the good man's streak of meanness, the great man's feet of clay. No one can read the Bible without knowing the worst about man, for even the best (our Lord excepted) are still far less than God-like. The verdict of one of the best of the Bible writers is short and straight: *All have sinned.* This is the way men are.

But there is another side to that. The Bible is anything but a mere rogues' gallery. There are genuine, authentic saints in it. Here we have stories of men who never were afraid of God in all their lives, but lived with him, in Chaucer's phrase, as "home-friends with the Lord." Here we read stories of men and women whose ideals, whose moral power and spiritual insight, soar far above our own.

If some reader, listening to Paul describing what it means, to him, to be a Christian, responds sadly, *"But I've never felt that way about it,"* Paul would say, "Don't you wish you could?" You can brush off Paul—if you insist on being so foolish—as an excitable man who has let his imagination run away with him; or you can face the reality of his experiences and seek that high level of reality yourself.

The other answer to this problem we have outlined is a more positive one. The Christian can point to Christ, and can say: "Any human experience, hope, aspiration, ideal, or motive which is in line with the character of Jesus is an experience I may rightly desire for my own. Any experience which is out of line with our Lord's character, which would have brought shame to him, should bring shame to me." So in this as in all other respects, Christ is the heart of the Bible.

The Bible as Revelation

Another kind of problem arises from the discovery of faith that the Bible is not only man's book, but God's. Arguments have taken place over the best formula for this discovery, this conviction about the Bible. Should we say the Bible *is* the Word of God, or that it *contains* the Word of God? We are not shut up to that *either-or*. We can also say that the Bible *conveys* the Word, and that it *becomes* the Word. All four of those statements are true, and it takes them all to express the full truth as the eye of faith sees it. If we say that the Bible contains the Word, we do not mean that the Word is inside it as an egg is inside a shell or a needle is in a haystack. We mean that the Bible contains the Word as an electric bulb contains light. The light shines from it, but still it is in it. And yet the bulb does not contain all the light there is. It does contain enough—even a flashlight contains enough light to walk by. If you break the bulb you do not destroy light, but without the bulb the light does go out. The bulb contains what is more precious than itself; so the revelation of God in the Bible is actually a greater thing than the book itself.

The Bible is also a sort of bridge, a channel, a telephone line, a wave length, along which the Word of God comes to us. The Bible *conveys* the Word from God to us. The Bible, moreover, *becomes* the Word in the sense that a sonata of Beethoven "becomes" music to the man who wakes up to it for the first time. Strictly speaking, the music does not change, it is what it always was; but one particular listener now hears what he once could not hear. Noise has become music. So the Bible, long a dead book to a non-reader, or even to a reader, may one day come alive, as the message from God to him. And when it does, it *is* the Word of God.

Is the Word of God, then, something created by faith? Can we say—must we say—that the Bible becomes the Word of God only to the man of faith? Asking that question is like asking whether Beethoven's music is music to a tone-deaf listener. The answer is a double one: yes and no. Beethoven's symphonies are just so much noise to the unmusical ear. He might as well have banged with a spoon on a tin pan, so far as such a listener is concerned. But just the same it is real music all the time, music waiting to be heard, music knocking at the ear's portal and singing, Let me in! So, in more than one place in the Bible we come upon that haunting phrase, "He that has ears to hear, let him hear." The music is always music—the Word is always the divine Word; but the music is not known to be music, it does not have the effect of music, without the hearing ear. So, for revelation to be complete, there has to be reception as well as utterance. The Word of God is no more than a rattling of syllables if there is none to *hear*. But to the ear and mind and heart of faith, the Bible conveys, becomes, and is (as Paul said of the Cross) the power and the wisdom of God.

Whether now we prefer to say that the Bible contains, or conveys, or becomes, or is the Word of God, we are saying that in it, in its various parts, and in many varied ways, God is making contact with us. Coleridge said, "The Bible finds me." A Christian can well go further and say, "God finds me, using the Bible to do it."

When we have said that the Bible is the Word of God, we have said that the Bible is *revelation*. But in saying this, we must think what we mean, or we shall be saying what we really do not intend. We—that is to say, the Church as a whole—should not be understood as meaning that every sentence in the Bible is revelation, taken by itself. To take a rather extreme example, we read (I Chron. 26:18) that "for the parbar on the west there were four at the road and two at the parbar." In the first place, nobody in the world now knows for certain what a parbar was; and in the second place, even if we did know, all this verse tells us is that there were two changes of guard a day at the parbar. Does this information bring us any nearer to God? Does it cast a light on our daily path? Of course not. It was evidently not intended to do so in the first place. In the same way you could go through the Bible picking out sentences here and there which are either totally obscure, or have nothing to say about God or the Christian life. (What value such parts of the Bible may have, we shall consider later on.)

Again, in calling the Bible a revelation we do not mean that every sentence in it makes known to us (or to the original author) in some supernatural manner, facts or propositions which could not possibly have been discovered by natural methods. For instance, Luke tells us that John the Baptist began to preach in the reign of Tiberius Caesar, and that Christ was born in the time of Augustus Caesar. The author gives no hint that an angel or the voice of God had told him these historical facts. Indeed, in the introduction to his Gospel (Luke 1:1-4) Luke's one claim is that he has investigated the whole matter and intends to set forth the facts in order. He makes no claim to have received his information by revelation. The Books of Chronicles, to take an Old Testament example, often refer to sources, but these are always library sources —that is, other books or records—and never supernatural sources of information.

Once more, in calling the Bible a revelation, the Church is divided on two questions. First, is the Bible the *only* revelation we have from God? The ancient and most widely held view is that it is not. Many Christian thinkers today are saying that it is. The editors and most writers of this Commentary hold to the older (and, we believe, the scriptural) view, namely that God is revealed in nature and the life of man; but that *saving* knowledge of God— that is to say, what we must know in order to find forgiveness and deliverance from our sins—comes to us through the Bible alone.

The other point on which the Church is divided is this: Does the revelation which the Bible brings us consist of propositions? If so, what are the propositions? And if not, what is there here instead of propositions? The view which probably everyone held at one time was that the revelation of the Bible does consist of propositions, disjointed parts, so to speak, of a system of doctrine which the Bible student has only to pick up and put together. Those who hold this view, however, do not agree on what, exactly, those propositions are. By this view, strictly held, a Christian is *one who believes a certain number of statements not believed by non-Christians*. Another view, now very widespread, holds that what is revealed in Scripture is not propositions, but primarily a Person, namely God himself: his character, his "history"—that is, his dealings with man in the past, climaxing in his self-revelation in Christ —and his purposes for mankind. By this view, a Christian is *one who believes in a certain Person in whom non-Christians do not believe*.

Suppose we attempt a provisional working definition of revelation which may include both these ideas. Let us say that there is something God knows which he wants men, or at least one man, to know. This "something God knows" may be a truth, or it may be an insight into the reason of things, or it may be—Himself. *The process by which God's knowledge becomes man's, is revelation.* This could include propositions, but it also includes, as its very center, the knowledge of Jesus Christ. God's revealing himself in Christ, God's action on behalf of the world through the birth, life, death, and resurrection of Christ, are not propositions, yet they are absolutely important as the center of revelation. On the other hand, however personal God's revelation may be, some propositions are inseparable from it.

Certainly, in spite of all the problems and difficulties, the Church has always accepted the Bible as a revelation, as *the* revelation, unique and indispensable.

Revelation and Inspiration

Revelation and inspiration are often confused with each other; but, although closely related, they are not the same. Revelation is basic, primary; inspiration is secondary. In the biblical sense there could be revelation without inspiration, but there can be no inspiration apart from revelation.

To understand their relationship, let us go back to the far-off days when the Bible was being written, and look at revelation and inspiration, so far as we may, in a particular case.

One of the best Bible definitions of revelation is in Hebrews 1:1 —"In many and various ways God spoke of old to our fathers by the prophets; but in these last days he has spoken to us by a Son." He spoke to our fathers, he has spoken to us—that is the favorite Bible word for it. We read that God spoke to Abraham. How did he speak? The famous Augustine, many centuries ago, when writing about this very point, remarked that it makes no difference whether the "speaking" was sound waves hitting Abraham's eardrums, or whether it was a vision, or a thought coming into his mind. The point is: God wanted Abraham to think something, and he thought it.

An illustration may take us a little farther. Consider one single sentence which is outstanding in the Bible: GOD IS LOVE. When you read that sentence in I John 4:8, you are looking at English printed words. But once upon a time there was no English language, when the handwritten Greek words meaning "God is love" were on a page of manuscript. That manuscript was a copy of another, and that of another, and so on back—until you come to a piece of papyrus on which the ink was still wet: *God is love.* Now at that moment, while the author was looking at his still unfinished page, that was the first time, so far as we know, that that sentence had ever been written down anywhere. It was written down then and there because the writer believed it. "God is love" was a thought in his mind before it was a sentence in a letter. *When the thought came to John's mind, and John believed it, revelation had taken place.*

Suppose the thought had crossed his mind but he had not believed it. Then there would have been no revelation. Why did John believe it, or how did he know it was true? It was not something he could prove; it is not something that can be disproved. Then how did he know it was true? There are two kinds of knowing. One is public knowing, knowledge that can be shared. If there are three chairs at the table, then anybody who says there are five, or two, is either crazy or blind. But it would be a mistake to say that anyone who does not think God is love is either crazy or blind. John's conviction is held by faith, not by demonstration. *Is it true?* If it is true, then John's faith is rewarded. Then John has penetrated to the heart of Reality itself; or rather God, who is himself supreme Reality, has penetrated *John.* This is revelation.

But now suppose John hesitates in his own mind: Shall I write this down? It is a bold sentence, no one ever said this before. It may be too hard to believe. We do not know whether John so hesitated or not. But we do know that something moved John to set down in black and white his faith-conviction that God is love. *That something-that-moved-John-to-write is inspiration.* Revelation—that is to say, original revelation—is the truth emerging in the mind of someone for the first time. Inspiration is the impulse to write it down, to make it permanent, to hand it on. But God is in both events, and each event needs the other. For without revelation there would be no point in inspiration. Without inspiration, on the other hand, revelation would die with the first person to whom it came.

But what about that sentence, "God is love"? Does it cease to be revelation when it is no longer a burning thought in the mind of the first man who ever believed it, and becomes words on a page? By no means. Inspiration—the impulse, divinely given, to preserve and communicate the revelation—is a kind of bridge between revelation and revelation. If a modern reader, through the influence of what John wrote, believes that God is love, then that writing, or printing, is for him an actual *revelation,* just as much as the original thought was to John.

The Bible as a Whole Is Revelation

Not all the Bible consists of sublime sentences like "God is love." We also read here that Uz was the brother of Buz, that one of David's wives was named Haggith, that Emmaus is about so far from Jerusalem, that Zabad and Aziza married foreign girls. If we are honest, we have to say that these statements are of no importance to us. That is, we not only can live ten years, we can live the rest of our lives without knowing them. To believe with all one's heart that God is love is a transforming experience. To believe with all one's heart that Uz and Buz were brothers or that Aziza's wife couldn't speak good Hebrew, is not transforming. Indeed, such facts cannot be believed with the whole heart; they aren't that kind of fact. They did not come to the original writer, we may gather, in a burst of light. They were public facts; he could have picked them up just by looking around him or by listening to village talk.

Our problem is: In what sense can we call these, and many other trivial matters of which the Bible speaks, "revelation"? They are certainly not revelation in the sense that they are hidden truths supernaturally made known. They are not at all in the class with "God is love" or "Thou art the Christ, the Son of the living God."

At this point we have to back away from the details and try to look at the larger picture. Remember what the Bible is—the Book of the acts of God. Remember its story line, the line that leads from man's beginnings to his final destiny; remember that Christ is the center of it all. What, above all, is revealed in the Bible? One Christian creed puts it in a simple but comprehensible way: It pleased God to reveal *himself,* and to declare *his will.* That is central; everything else is incidental. God's nature and character, and what he wants us to do—that is what the Bible writers as a whole perceived, believed, and in their various ways wrote down. Many details emerge in the telling of the great story which are in themselves unimportant. Nothing whatever hinges on them; it would be making a mountain out of a molehill to call them supernatural.

Still there is something more, to which a parallel may be found by falling in love. If a woman has opened her heart to a man who loves her, the single sentence "I love you" glows with beauty and surprise. It is, on the human level, a transforming revelation. But along with it go many unimportant facts. This girl has an uncle named Bill, she likes oatmeal for breakfast, she weighs 125 pounds, she plays the accordion by ear, her hair is a certain shade of auburn, she used to go to public school in Hackensack—and so on, and so on. If the man doesn't love the girl, listening to all those things only bores him. But now that they love each other, to everything she tells him he answers, "Tell me more." It is all interesting because it is all part of the story of one who loves him.

So there is much in the Bible which is unimportant in itself, and which is "revelation" only because it is part of the story of how God has been working out his great purposes in the world. *Apart from* the story of salvation such details are hardly worth reading. As *a part of* the story of salvation, they gleam with some reflected light.

Revelation Is Gradual

There are still problems that bother many readers of the Bible, particularly believing readers. What about things in the Bible which are really ungodly, any way you take them? There are, for example, some cursing Psalms. The author of Psalm 137 rejoices to think of enemy babies having their heads bashed against a rock. The author of Psalm 69 also prays against his enemies; he asks God never to forgive them. Psalm 109 prays for the death of the Psalmist's enemy, prays that the enemy's children may be beggars, and that none may take pity on them. The Psalmist even prays that his enemy's father and mother may never have their sins forgiven. All this is far from Christian. If we are Christians we know we have no right to make such thoughts our own. Then how can it be revelation? The same can be said about Samuel's killing Agag, and condemning Saul for sparing the lives of babies and not committing total genocide—killing an entire race—today regarded as a serious crime.

For particular problems, these and others, the reader must consult the commentary. In general, we should be honest and confess that such things are not only pre-Christian, they are sub-Christian. We get into great moral confusion if we pretend otherwise. Such examples, however, may help us to realize that revelation is not sudden and complete; it is gradual. These ancient men of religion believed in the true God, but they had not yet fully understood his will. The revelation of God and his will, in the Bible, is like the growing light at sunrise; the first glimmers of dawn are more dark than bright, yet it is genuine light. The dark is destined to dwindle, the dawn light will grow in Christ to the perfect day.

Another thought that comes in here is this: Such parts of the Bible as are plainly sub-Christian should be compared, not only with the full light of the Gospels, but also with the customs, ideals, and laws of other peoples in those ancient times. The law given in the opening verses of Deuteronomy 24, on divorce, is sub-Christian, and Jesus repudiated it. But the reason why it was not a better law—that is, why it was not a law which more truly expressed God's ideal for marriage—was not that God was sub-Christian! It was because of the "hardness of heart" of the people. *They* were sub-Christian. It was the best law possible under the circumstances. Furthermore, if we compare this and other Hebrew laws with those of other peoples in that far-off time, we find the laws of the Hebrews as a whole distinctly, even startlingly, on a higher moral plane than those of their neighbors. They had not arrived, but they were on their way—God's way.

How Did God Inspire the Bible?

All branches of the Christian Church, and all schools of Christian thought, agree that God did inspire the Bible. But inspiration is understood in various ways. Two extreme views are very seldom held, but should be mentioned, if only to show what is wrong with them. One is that the inspiration of Scripture, what has been called here the urge-to-write, is no different from the urge-to-write that any author has; and that, therefore, there is no real difference between the Bible and any other collection of writings, so far as inspiration is concerned. There is a distinct difference, however, at two points. One point of difference is found in the quality of the inspired writers of the Bible. A New Testament writer calls them "holy men of old." They were peculiarly sensitive to the presence and the will of God. We can hardly think of a Moses and a Mencken as inspired in the same way, however brilliant Mencken may have been. Furthermore, there is a difference in what men are inspired to write. The Bible writers' concern was with the story of salvation. If we may draw a parallel, two persons may have the urge-to-shout. But can we say that the urge-to-shout of an evangelist is precisely the same as the urge-to-shout of a drunken sailor? So the urge-to-write was, with the Bible writers, the urge-to-write *this,* the Bible. That the book which they collectively produced is unique, suggests that their inspiration was unique.

At the other end of the line from the above is a different theory of inspiration: namely, that God dictated the whole Bible, the writers being no more than pens in the Holy Spirit's hand. Not many thoughtful Christians can go along with this. Such a theory would make God responsible for misspellings and for bad grammar, to say nothing of errors in geography and zoology and the like, such as locating the sources of the Nile (the "Gihon") and the Euphrates in the same spot (Gen. 2:10), asserting that the hare chews the cud (Lev. 11:6), or classifying the bat as a bird (Lev. 11:13-19). And how could we say that God dictated personally the sub-Christian elements in the Old Testament? For reasons such as these, almost no theologians in our times will say that inspiration means dictation.

Somewhere between these extremes must be the truth, and the Christian Church is not all of one mind about it. A widely held view connects inspiration and providence. A person who believes in prayer and in providence should have no great difficulty with inspiration. A belief in prayer and in providence implies a belief that God himself operates as a force, indeed the deciding force in this world. No one can tell *how* God does so, but Christians believe that he does. So we can believe that God moves men to write without professing to know just how. We may well believe that when God wants, let us say, the Gospel by Matthew to be written, he raises up a man who will of his own accord prepare and write just such a book. At all events, however the biblical writers got it, the urge-to-write was there, and God was in that urge, because the writing was what he intended.

Inerrancy

If God inspired the Bible, by whatever means, does that eliminate mistakes of every kind? Some Christians say yes. Anything God does must be flawless; there is neither evil nor error in it. He would not put his priceless revelation into a form to be handed down through the centuries, unless that form itself were perfect. So the Bible is without error of any kind. Some parts of it may be more important than others, and more valuable, but no part is more true than any other, for it is all one hundred per cent true.

Other Christians find it impossible to subscribe to this view. They do not find it in the Bible itself. Further, nothing God does on this planet by the agency of man is flawless; not even his Church is without blemish. Whatever human beings, even saintly ones, have to do with is tinged with imperfection; can the Bible be an exception? True, the Holy Spirit is in the Bible; but the Holy Spirit is also in Christians, and even the Apostle Peter, after Pentecost, could still make mistakes and commit sin. But the real reason why those Christians who cannot agree with the doctrine of inerrancy have given it up is not a theoretical reason at all. It is the very practical one: they find errors there. One single error in the Bible shatters the theory of inerrancy past repair. The efforts to defend the errors, to show that they are actually and literally true and right, requires so many over-ingenious twists and turns, that many of those who hold to an absolutely errorless Bible will not affirm that the Bible as we have it is without error. They claim such a quality only for the lost originals. Those who cannot accept the doctrine of inerrancy can only say to this: The only Bible we have, the only one about which we can talk realistically, is not this alleged flawless original. It is close enough to the original, so that we have good reason to believe there is very little difference indeed. But in any case, it was evidently not God's intention that *we* should have a flawless Bible, whatever the original may have been. The saving truth of God comes to us in imperfect translations of an imperfect Hebrew and Greek text.

Two questions may help the reader find his way beyond all the argument over inerrancy. One question is this: Can God make truth known through fiction? Some people would indignantly say, No! God can speak only through the most literal and precise factual propositions. God is the God of fact, not of fiction. Further thought, however, would discover that all Christians, including those who are so horrified by the notion of "fiction" in the Bible, in any form, accept every day some things in the Bible which are not literally true. Jesus is called the Lamb of God; but he was a human being, not a quadruped. God is called a Rock; is that fact or fiction? It is fiction, strictly speaking; but the word conveys a truth about God. "Factually" speaking, God is no more a senseless piece of rock than Jesus is a baby sheep. In II Samuel the poet speaks of God as blowing with the "breath of his nostrils"; does God actually have a nose and lungs? Readers of the Bible are seldom bothered by such expressions. They are expressive fictions, fictions that carry true meanings. It is no more a reflection on the honesty of God to take Jonah, for example, as an inspired work of fiction, than it is to take "Lamb of God" as an inspired figure of speech.

Somebody may say, at this point, Now I am getting all mixed up. How can I tell what is literal and what is poetic, figurative, or fictional? The best answer is: Use your common sense. What might be called a "gentleman's rule" of interpreting anyone's words is to take them literally unless there is good reason to take them otherwise; but where there is good reason to take them otherwise, then it is stupid to take them literally. To see how this works, the reader must consult a commentary on passages about which he is puzzled —always remembering that no commentary can claim to be infallible! Consider in this light the early chapters of Genesis, the Books of Jonah, Esther, and the Psalms, and the parables of Jesus. Some readers may conclude that God not only can, but does, convey powerful truth through stories which may never have "happened" at all.

The other question is a more important one: What, after all, is the *purpose* of the Bible? What is the heart of the Bible? What is it that gives the Bible its power and its value, and makes it penetrating and precious? We have already seen what this is: the revelation of God himself, and his will for mankind. This is the clue that leads us past all difficulties, this is the direction marker that does not lead us astray. The great saints who have found in the Bible the very Word of God, who have been rebuked, humbled, enlightened, cheered, and changed by the Bible, because they have found Christ there, and have found life in him—these people have not been bothered about the habits of rabbits or whether the bat is a bird. To deny that the Bible as we have it has a single error of any kind is rather like denying that one's mother ever sinned. But to keep looking and looking for mistakes in the Bible is like forever pointing out all the mistakes one's mother made. A univac makes no mistakes; mothers do. But only a mother can give us life.

Who Sponsors the Bible?

A very disturbing problem occurs to some people, although most people never think of it. Who has, or had, the right to say what books belong in the Bible? Luke tells us that many gospels existed in his day. Why were our four selected from the many, and who selected them? For every prophet there was a horde of false prophets. For every letter preserved to us in the New Testament there must have been many others not kept. Somebody did some picking and choosing. Somebody, some individual or some committee, must have put the label "Bible" on this collection and shoved the rest aside. Who did this, what right had they to do it, and how do we know they were right?

This is called the problem of the *Canon*. This word (only one "n" in the middle, please) as applied to our Bible, or the Bible of any other religion, means a list of books which are accepted by the (or a) Church as carrying divine authority and, therefore, as a standard for religious faith and for moral practice. How was this list made up? How was the cream of the Canon skimmed off from the milk of other similar literature?

The final seal of approval was usually given by some council or convocation of men recognized in the Church as leaders with authority. But before any final decision, there was a long period of time during which the Canon was growing.

Few if any books of the Bible were in the Canon, that is to say, officially adopted as part of Scripture, immediately on being written. It was not as simple as that. The Canon has a history. While we do not know all the details, we do know there were certain stages in the process.

After a book had been written—a hymnbook, a collection of laws, a small volume of sermons, whatever it might be—hand-made copies would circulate here and there, and the book would make its own appeal to its readers. The second stage would be the use of the book in public worship. The process would work both ways: the growing popular appeal to the minds and hearts of men would lead to its use in worship, and the public and solemn use of the book would induce more and more people to read it. Finally some council of recognized authority would officially and formally approve what the people of God had already unofficially and informally done, namely, accept the book, or books, as God's Word.

Neither the Old nor the New Testament was canonized all at once. In the Old Testament the first general group of books to be so recognized was the Pentateuch, about 400 B.C. Sometime later, say by 200 B.C., the books of the Prophets (which the Jews understood to include the "historical" books) were included in the Canon; and finally, not long before the time of Christ, the other books known as the "Writings" were accepted. (These were Psalms,

Proverbs, Job, Song of Solomon, Ruth, Lamentations, Ecclesiastes, Esther, Daniel, Ezra-Nehemiah, and Chronicles.) Thus the Old Testament Canon was fixed; that is to say, by the time of Christ the Jewish leaders and people had officially acknowledged its divine authority. For a while, even after the time of Christ, there was some question in regard to a few books, notably Ecclesiastes and the Song of Solomon. But after the Council of Jamnia in the first century A.D. there were no further debates among Jews about what was Scripture and what was not. Jews who read Hebrew from then on had the same sacred books that we find in our Protestant Old Testament, except that they were differently arranged. Jewish Christians who knew Hebrew likewise had in their Old Testament the same books we have in ours today. Greek-speaking Christians had a larger Bible than we have.

The process also was gradual in the history of the New Testament Canon. Some books, like our four Gospels, were widely accepted almost as soon as written, and had no serious rivals; other books took longer to be circulated, and to be adopted and used in public worship. There is definite evidence that by A.D. 170 the Church at large had accepted all the New Testament books we now have, excepting Hebrews, III John, I and II Peter. There were differences of opinion about the Letter of James and the Book of Revelation. The official "fixing" of the Canon, that is to say the final listing of Christian writings which were Scripture for the Church, was done by a number of councils, beginning near the end of the fourth century after Christ. These councils, however, simply made official what the Church had already accepted and had been using. The councils approved the books which large city churches had been using for years in public worship. These churches, in turn, had been using those particular books because Christian people had long found them to be sources of spiritual comfort and power. What the councils did was to ratify the spiritual insight of the rank and file of the Church. It is not true that any convocation of bishops forced the Bible on the Church, made them swallow it, as it were. On the contrary, the Church, the great mass of Christians, without pressure from priests or bishops, had already found these books to contain spiritual food.

Why is the Roman Catholic Bible larger than the Protestant Bible? The answer goes back to the second century before Christ, or about that time. The Old Testament was then being translated for the first time into a foreign language. That other language was

Greek, which at the time was used by more Jews than was Hebrew. No one knows all about what happened, but we do know that when that Greek translation was completed (the name for it is the Septuagint), the old arrangement of books had been changed, new names had been given to some books, and (most radical change) a number of books had been added, or inserted, which were not in the Hebrew Canon.

Of course the people who wrote the New Testament in Greek, and the people who read it, would also read their Old Testament in Greek. The form of the Old Testament familiar to most Christians thus became the Septuagint—that is, the Greek Canon, with its additional books.

Now the books which appeared first in the Greek Canon of the Old Testament, roughly speaking, are called as a group the Apocrypha. Some leaders in the Early Church, notably Jerome, doubted whether they ought to be in the Christian Bible. But the Christian Church kept them and regarded them as inspired, until the time of the Reformation. At that time, after some discussion, the Protestants gradually rejected the Apocrypha, every bit; whereas the Roman Church declared that it was all inspired, as much so as the rest of the Bible. Thus the Protestants went back to the Hebrew Canon, while the Roman Church to this day holds to the Greek Canon, and so has a longer Bible than the Protestants.

The Authority of the Bible

We must ask one more question. By what authority do we accept the authority of the Bible? To that question, the only answer which makes sense is to declare that the Bible is its own authority. Any endorsement of it from outside would be like a committee endorsing God. God does not need references. Neither does God's Word. A church, a bishop, a council, which would guarantee the Bible for us is really setting itself up above the Bible as a jury to judge it. The Christian conviction has always been that the Bible judges *us*.

The word of a man may need the word of a more highly placed man to verify it. But there is no more highly placed God. Who, after all, selected *these* books as Scripture? It was done first of all by the collective judgment of everyday Christians who discovered that these books found *them*. All who read and love the Bible feel by instinct what certain theologians have put into more formal words: *the final witness to the truth and authority of the Bible is the same Holy Spirit under whose inspiration it was written.*

We can put this in another way: How do we know the Bible is inspired? If we can be convinced of that, then of course it carries authority. But how do we know it? Not by argument. Not even the most learned theologian in Christendom can sit at a table with you and demonstrate that the Bible is inspired. The inspiration and authority of the Bible have to be discovered, not announced.

Suppose, for instance, you did not believe that Johann Sebastian Bach wrote great music? How could I prove to you that he did? I could hire a hall and employ an orator to make a speech every seven days telling you what a great musician Bach was. I could form a musical club, and keep you out, or put you out, if you would not admit that Bach wrote great music. But that would not satisfy you. It ought not to satisfy you. Study Bach for yourself. Listen to his music. Play some of it, if you have the skill. Let those soul-shaking harmonies possess you. Then you will know. And once you have discovered what Bach's music is, no cheap criticism, no sneers that he has been outmoded, will shake you from what you know to be true.

Do you want to know whether the Bible has authority? Do you want to know whether it is inspired? Do not listen to theologians telling you about it. Listen to the Word yourself. Go sit in a quiet place and hear the harmonies of God. It is true, some never hear, being spiritually tone deaf. But those who have an ear, those in whose minds is the true resonance, once they have passed within sound of the music of the marching saints, will ever after have some overtones of heaven in their souls.

THE HISTORY OF THE
PEOPLE OF GOD

The Bible is *one story* which can be told two ways. The *one story* can be told as the story of God's loving purpose, or it can be told as the story of the people of God, people who were called and drawn by him in an especially important way, people through whom God's purpose has been, is being, and will be worked out to its final fulfillment. In this article the story will be traced from the side of the people of God, and therefore it must be told as *history,* for the people lived in the world and took part in its happenings. The special people of God, whose story is told in the Bible, did not live in a vacuum, but were always involved in the course of history. The particular events and the particular persons appearing in the Bible must always be seen in relationship to other events and other characters which may not be a part of the biblical story as such.

At the same time, it must be realized that telling the story of the Bible as history does not mean that the mere recital of happenings and relationships in themselves is to be taken as the Word of God. It is the *meaning* of the events, the interpretation which is attached to them, reflected in the way the events are remembered and recounted, that makes this particular series of happenings and this particular succession of individuals and groups the channel through which the Word of God came to men, and through which the same Word still comes to us.

This means, then, that in reading or studying the story of the Bible it is helpful to think of three things: the *setting* of the story, the *story* itself, and the *meaning* of the story. By "setting" is meant the actual situation and events contemporary with the biblical history. To be aware of this helps one understand some of the special implications of the story itself; it helps also to remind one that this was not just a "story" but actual happenings in an actual world. By the "story" is meant the main line of the history in which the people of God came to understand his will and his purpose for them and for the world. Not all of the story can be told, but there

are certain outstanding features through which can be traced the
one ongoing purpose of God. By "meaning" is meant the important insights and ideas which were found in the happenings themselves and for the sake of which the history was recollected and
passed on.

Before the actual history is begun, it will be necessary to look
briefly at the setting of the *entire* story. In this connection constant
reference should be made to a good atlas of the Bible, or at least
to a good map of the biblical lands.

The Setting of the Whole Story

General

The story of God's people, since it did take place in the world,
is one that involves particular places and particular times. The actual geographical situation within which the people of God moved
affected to some extent their entire life and history.

The setting was a narrow one, judged by miles alone. With few
exceptions the world of the Old Testament could be included in a
rectangle 500 miles north to south, and 1000 miles east to west.
Much of the area thus enclosed, moreover, was uninhabitable. To
describe the actual world of the Old Testament one needs first of
all to draw a large figure "S," inclined to the right, with the upper
arm considerably longer than the lower. The bottom arm would
represent Egypt, the middle bar the land of Palestine, and the upper arm the lands of the Mesopotamian region.

The figure must be drawn this way, of course, because of two
formidable barriers to trade and to the development of stable
civilization. The one, around which the bottom arm of the "S"
curves, is the Mediterranean Sea; the other, within the top curve,
is the great desert. Sea and desert so greatly restricted movements
of trade and so excluded settled life that for all intents and purposes civilization and history moved within a narrow confine
stretching from the Nile Valley and the Delta of Egypt, up across
the Sinai Peninsula, hugging the coast, through the lands of Palestine and Syria, and back southward again through the valley of
the "two rivers," to the Persian Gulf. This narrow strip of land,
not much over 100 miles in width at any place, much narrower at
most, comprised the setting for the largest part of the history of
God's people.

All three parts of this world, Egypt, Palestine and Syria, and

Mesopotamia illustrate the vital necessity of adequate water supply. Egypt is still, as it was then, the Valley and the Delta of the Nile River; Palestine is arable and inhabitable largely because the prevailing winds from the Mediterranean drop their rain on the west slope of the mountains which parallel the seacoast; Mesopotamia is the fertile delta-like region between the Tigris and the Euphrates Rivers. In these areas some stability of life was possible, and here rose the two great centers of early civilization, Egypt and Mesopotamia, with Palestine and Syria hung like a bridge between.

Two other sections, outside this strip of land which served as the locale of civilization, need to be considered in the history of the people of God. One is the great land plateau which is the Arabian Peninsula. This body of land was the original home of all the Semitic people who, migrating periodically from the relatively infertile peninsula, settled and developed the Mesopotamian region and Syria and Palestine. The other section, lying outside the narrow strip, was the region later known as Asia Minor, the home of Indo-European peoples who in a more indirect way also affected the lives and fortunes of the people of the Old Testament. This area was of great importance in the time of the New Testament and will be considered later.

Geography of Palestine

The central part of the land strip, the bridge between the two great centers of world power, demands a closer look. What is known as Palestine is a small area, not over 150 miles "from Dan to Beersheba"—that is, from the north to the south—and not much over 40 miles in width. There is a coastal plain with three main sections, from north to south, the Plain of Acco, the Plain of Sharon, and the Plain of Philistia. In the center of the land is a line of hills rising to 4000 feet in the north, continuing through the central region of Samaria and the hills of Judah, and dropping off to the south.

The Jordan Valley is part of a great rift stretching from Syria down through Palestine to the Red Sea and finally into Africa. The Jordan River rises at Mount Hermon, flows through Lake Huleh, then through the Sea of Galilee where it is 685 feet below sea level, and empties into the Dead Sea at 1290 feet below the sea. To the east there is the plateau of Transjordan, comprising sections such as Bashan, Gilead, Moab, and Edom.

The Age of the Patriarchs

The Setting

The biblical history of the patriarchal period focuses at the first on the story of one man, Abraham. The time was somewhere about the beginning of the second millennium B.C., that is, around 2000 B.C.

So far as Mesopotamia and Egypt are concerned, civilization had stretched far behind this time. Europe was still in the dimness of "prehistory" at the beginning of the second millennium, but there had been great urban cultures in the Babylonian area for two thousand years before Abraham. In the third millennium had come a period of high culture with extensive literary activity in Mesopotamia, and in Egypt a civilization with a massive central power symbolized in the pyramids which were constructed during the last half of the millennium.

The time from 2000 to 1700 B.C. found the lands of the fertile strip invaded by successive waves of Semitic people from the Arabian Peninsula. The entire region, including Egypt, was profoundly affected by these invasions so that there came radical changes in culture and in politics.

The Story

The biblical story proper begins with events in the life of a wandering Semite during the period sketched above. From Ur, a center of Babylonian culture, he moved to Haran, one of the areas particularly affected by Semitic invasion. From here Abraham and his kinsmen journeyed on into Palestine where he lived for the remainder of his life. His ceaseless wanderings throughout the land are evidence of his nomadic occupation.

In Palestine were born and lived two generations of Abraham's descendants. Finally in a time of famine they departed to Egypt where they were welcomed as settlers by the rulers of Egypt. The Book of Genesis is mainly concerned with selected incidents in the lives of Abraham, Isaac, Jacob, and Joseph, that is, four generations of these nomadic herdsmen during the three centuries from 2000 to 1700 B.C.

The Meaning of the Story

The meaning and importance of this story are partly involved in the fact that it follows, in the Bible, a great prologue, to which this simple history of wandering Semites is connected. In the opening chapters of the Bible there are set forth the fact of God's creation of the world and all of life, the fact of God's purpose, the fact of mankind's refusal to accept the position and destiny for which God created him, and the fact of God's continuing concern with man. Here, too, are shown the effects of mankind's sin, as it grows to an infection that spreads through all of life, extending to each individual and as well to the whole corporate life of men and nations.

This background gives to the story of Abraham and all his successors a special meaning. For they are seen to be the ones with whom God began to deal in a special way; they were the particular people through whom he was to work out his purpose for all. In the stories of the patriarchs is seen also the *way* in which God was to work with his people. Here were recipients of God's grace. They were men and women called by God to be partakers of a covenant of love and hope and, at the same time, to serve as instruments of his will.

It is evident, from the honest and unflinching narrative of Genesis, that the essential meaning of the partriarchal stories does not lie in the character of the people. They are not remembered and cherished because of their value as moral examples. They were not plaster saints but real people, sinners in need of God and drawn by him into a relationship of security and love, to which their true response was faith alone. This relationship is what makes them important; and so clear in the lives of these early men are the issues of God's call and offer, and man's response to God in faith and life, that these patriarchal narratives are regarded as forming one of the crucial parts of the story of God's whole purpose in and for the world.

The Exodus

The Setting

The Book of Genesis closes with the departure of the descendants of Abraham for Egypt where they settled in the land of Goshen, there to live for four centuries, during which time they greatly increased in numbers. During these four centuries we know almost nothing about these people beyond the simple fact of numerical increase.

The centuries were not, however, a time of inactivity in the affairs of the world. Egypt, the scene of the later Exodus, was invaded about 1710 B.C. by an alien people from Asia known as *Hyksos* or "foreign rulers." These people, largely of Semitic origin, established a powerful empire, the boundaries of which included Palestine and Syria. The biblical account of Joseph's extraordinary power in Egypt fits well with the rule of the "foreign kings."

During the following centuries, while the Hebrews lived in Egypt, the reign of the Hyksos was brought to an end by native rulers of Upper Egypt. Meanwhile other nations were also undergoing change. The Babylonian Empire was itself broken by an alien people, the Kassites, and for four centuries exerted no great influence in the affairs of the western countries. Other important empires of the period were that of Mitanni, an Indo-Iranian and Hurrian people controlling a large area northeast of Palestine, and that of the Hittites in eastern Asia Minor.

When the Hittites began to press into the lands of Mitanni and the Egyptian Empire in Syria and Palestine, Egypt was undergoing a period of internal weakness and, as a consequence, lost much of her empire. Under Seti I and Rameses II, however, there were attempts to regain the lost territory, with resulting warfare, particularly during the fourteenth and thirteenth centuries.

During this period hostility to Semitic people in Egypt was on the increase. At the same time, with the expansion of empire and the demands of war there came greater need for slave labor. The Hebrew peoples, living on the borders of Egypt, were gradually reduced to the status of slaves, their numbers severely curtailed in fear that they might rebel, or at least serve as an open invitation to invasion from outside the empire.

By the labors of these Hebrew slaves the rulers of the Nineteenth Dynasty in Egypt built the cities of Pithom and Rameses, probably completed during the reign of Seti I. The sites of both have been discovered in comparatively recent times.

About the middle of the thirteenth century, when the biblical story takes up again, Rameses II was engaged in warfare in Palestine and Syria, seeking to regain his empire. Palestine itself was inhabited by the Canaanites of the Bible.

The Story

In Egypt there appeared a leader for the dispossessed Hebrew people. His name, Moses, was given him by the daughter of Pharaoh, and he had been reared in the royal palace, although he was himself a Hebrew. After once endangering his life in defense of a fellow Hebrew he had fled for safety from Egypt into the wilderness of the Sinai Peninsula, where he had lived for a considerable time with the family of Jethro, a priest of Midian. There Moses had had an experience which had sent him back to Egypt to the aid of his own people. In Sinai he had come into meeting with God, the God of his patriarchal ancestors, and this God had commissioned him to lead the Hebrews out of Egypt, through the wilderness of Sinai, and finally into Canaan, the land of their forefathers.

Such a venture, of course, aroused the opposition of Egypt, and Moses' struggle with the power of the nation was not easily won. Unwilling to lose such a valuable supply of cheap labor, Pharaoh resisted, one after the other, the threatening signs which Moses gave him. Then, in a single night, the first-born of the houses of Egypt were killed, and the Hebrews, their houses miraculously passed over by the destruction, rose up and fled from the land.

When they were pursued by the hosts of Egypt they came to what seemed to be a dead end, as they arrived at an arm of the Red Sea. But there they were delivered again as the water opened for them and they passed over in safety, and as it closed to destroy their pursuers. From the Red Sea they came by short stages to "Mount Sinai," somewhere in the peninsula. There they, like Moses before them and their ancestors centuries earlier in different lands, came face to face with God—the very God who had acted in their behalf by delivering them from the land of darkness and death and bringing them along the way to the land of promise.

The Meaning of the Story

To this Exodus from Egypt the people of Israel looked back forever after. It marked the beginning of those singular happenings which made them what they were as a nation. It was for them, first of all, an experience of the grace of God, and thus it served to define the nature of the God with whom they had to do. He was a God of grace and of loving concern. They had not been chosen because of any superiority of their own. They were not mighty, they were not great in number; they were, in fact, slaves, without hope, and without real life. But to them God had come. And he had come before any act on their part. No matter what they did thereafter, they could never deserve the grace of God, for he had been "long beforehand" with them; they could not anticipate God.

They saw this grace of God, moreover, in all the details of the Exodus. The powers of oppression had been stayed in their behalf. In all the happenings that confounded the Egyptians, the people of Israel had been strangely unaffected and untouched. And when they had sat through the Passover night, a pilgrim people, ready to move at the command of the Lord, they had known again what grace was, as the Destroyer had passed them by. And then, when they had come to the Red Sea, to a disaster which seemed to be the end of hope itself, they had been met with grace and redemption. God had acted for them. This is what the Exodus meant, above everything else.

It was also true that God had acted in a certain way. He did not act for them or speak to them in a separate, isolated series of purely heavenly events, but in the very life in which they lived. He had acted in Egypt, the Egypt of the Nineteenth Dynasty, meeting and destroying the powers of that nation. He had acted in the cities and homes in which they lived, on the roads of Egypt, at the edge of the Red Sea. The people, then, not only came face to face with *a* god at Sinai, they came face to face with *the* God of grace, who worked in the actual affairs of men and who could be known in the events of men's lives.

The Covenant

The Setting

The Israelites were led out of Egypt for a purpose, the meaning of which became clear as they came to Mount Sinai, somewhere in the peninsula of Sinai. This is a triangular body of land, some 250 miles in length and 140 miles in width at the base in the north. Into this peninsula the people moved following their escape at the Red Sea. After a short journey, they came to a mountain, the exact location of which is uncertain. The oldest tradition places it at the southern tip of the peninsula, and this seems to be confirmed by the location of the stations along the way of the journey.

The Israelites lived in this same peninsula for a full generation, after they had made a start toward Palestine with the evident intent of invading it from the south, only to be turned back by fear of the inhabitants of the land.

The Story

The Book of Exodus tells how the Israelites, delivered by God from Egypt, and sustained by him along the way as he provided their food, came to Mount Sinai. There they were confronted with some kind of upheaval of nature, with threatening light and fire, with smoke and sounds of thunder. The description sounds at times like a description of volcanic activity, at others like a severe windstorm.

In this event they recognized that God was speaking to them, defining the purpose for which they had been delivered, and calling them into a peculiar way of life growing out of a covenant relation with him. The offer of the Covenant was made by God and was accepted by the people in solemn acts of consecration, probably involving a communal meal and a ritual of sacrifice. The conditions of the Covenant were given them, including a code of laws which were to govern their life thereafter, and including also the gracious promise of God's perpetual blessing to them and, through them, to other peoples.

The Meaning of the Story

In a real sense Mount Sinai casts its shadow over the entire Old Testament, for the Covenant was the most important feature of Israel's life. The idea of the Covenant so fixed itself upon them and their life that the Israelite people became henceforth the people of the Covenant, people bound in a peculiar and intimate relationship to God.

The term "covenant" needs definition, for in modern usage it tends to stand for "contract" or even "bargain." In the case of the Covenant at Sinai, although there were certainly elements of mutual responsibility, from first to last it was a sign of God's gracious dealings with men. It was not a bargain made by the nation with God. They did not come to Sinai to bargain, they had already been chosen by God, redeemed by him, led by him into this covenant relation. It was not *their* covenant at all, but *God's* Covenant.

The Covenant, moreover, defined a way of life, so that their relationship to God was not simply a matter of being delivered by him, but also a whole new way of living. In the regulations of the Covenant, included in chapters 20-23 of the Book of Exodus, there are provisions that relate both to social and to religious matters. In the Covenant men found that they had responsibility to their fellow men and at the same time responsibility to God. Religion and social relationships were bound into one way of life, so that division between the two would be unthinkable.

The law which was given to guide covenant response on the part of the people strongly suggested an obligation to see that national, social, and religious activities would all somehow grow out of and reflect the knowledge of God. The Covenant established Israel as a peculiar people, but their peculiarity was not so much that they did or did not do certain things. Rather, their whole way of life was to be a testimony to the grace and mercy, the justice and righteousness, of God. In this way, the Israelites would be a powerful witness to all the world, a witness to God, as the life of the nation would be held up as a mirror for all the world to see, a mirror reflecting the image of God.

The Covenant was also an undergirding for the future, and thus it set a basis for security and assurance. God pledged himself for the years that were to come, and men found thereby that they could act and live in the present with assurance. Their future standing with God was seen to be dependent upon God, not upon themselves; least of all was it dependent upon the contingent and accidental facts of their own life and response. The future was God's, the outworking of his own unconditional grace.

The Conquest

The Setting

The most probable date for the Exodus of the Israelites from Egypt is sometime in the reign of Rameses II (about 1290 B.C.). Allowing for the sojourn of forty years in the wilderness following the first unsuccessful attempt to invade Palestine from the south, we may assume that the events which make up most of the story in the Book of Joshua took place between 1250 and 1225 B.C. Although there are some difficulties involved in these dates they appear to agree with the main features of the biblical narrative and with the main archaeological evidence concerning the conquest of Palestine.

What was the situation during the thirteenth century B.C., that is, during the time when the Israelites were living as nomads in Sinai and were, later, infiltrating and invading Palestine? During the first part of the century Egypt was still struggling for recapture of her control over Palestine and Syria. For a time the chief opponents were the Hittites, but wars between these two nations were brought to an end in 1270 B.C. The treaty which marked the end of warfare probably also reflects the rising power of Assyria and her increasing threat to the eastern section of the Hittite Empire. During the remainder of the century Egypt still exercised some control over Palestine, but was in a period of decline. At the end of the century, in a poem celebrating Pharaoh Merenptah's victories, there is a mention of Israel in Palestine.

During the thirteenth century came the conquest of the land of Palestine by the tribes that had been delivered from Egypt. It began as a strong military campaign, but was undoubtedly helped along by resident Israelites who were bound to their brothers by tradition, and possibly by a Covenant theology. Although the conquest was incomplete in many places it was thorough enough to allow for consolidation and gradual settlement of the land.

During the next two centuries both Egypt and the Mesopotamian region were comparatively quiescent so that there were no major campaigns in Palestine to hinder the growth of the Israelite nation.

The Canaanite dwellers, many of whom had been undisturbed by the Conquest, or had held out against it, enjoyed a much higher level of culture than did the Israelites. Their cities were wealthy and well fortified in comparison to the crude settlements built up by the conquerors.

To the east were the kingdoms of Moab and Ammon, which had been left untouched by the invaders. Canaan had always been in danger of attack from these hostile neighbors, and the first two centuries of Israel's life in the land were no exception. From time to time, as the story indicates, these nomadic people would subjugate some part of the land, and appropriate its produce.

About the middle of this period there appeared a major threat, posed by the arrival of the Philistines in the area. These were people from the Greek islands, including Crete, who had been displaced by great barbarian movements in Europe pressing down into the Mediterranean lands. Driven back in their attempt to settle along the borders of Egypt, these seafaring peoples invaded the southern part of Canaan, settling along the seacoast and building up a confederacy of five cities.

With the arrival of the Philistines the Iron Age came to Palestine. Up to this time copper had been the major metal, although it had long been combined with tin to make bronze. But iron, a superior metal for instruments of war and agriculture, though known, had not been used, since the secret of smelting it had been guarded by the Hittites. The Philistines undoubtedly were able to smelt iron, and this ability, along with their superior civilization in general, gave them considerable advantage over the Israelite tribes.

The Story

Putting together the account in the Books of Joshua and Judges and the best available evidence from archaeology, two conclusions may be reached with fair certainty. The first is that there was a considerable body of Israelites who were in the land of Palestine before the actual arrival of the tribes who had been in Egypt. These could have been descendants of original Israelite families who did not go into Egypt, or of Israelites driven out of Egypt with the expulsion of the Hyksos, or of groups that had left Egypt earlier—for example, some who had returned at the time of the burial of Jacob.

The second conclusion is that the actual conquest of the land by the Israelites under Joshua took place in three well-defined stages. The first is chronicled in the Book of Numbers, where there is the account of a new generation of Israelites, reared in the desert, with a vigor born of their desert life, who were led by Moses into the region east of the River Jordan, defeating Sihon and Og on the way. This stage ended with Israel in control of the central part of the Transjordan country.

The second stage of the Conquest is told in the early chapters of Joshua, and deals with the subjugation of the central section of Palestine itself. It begins with the crossing of the Jordan and the fall of the city of Jericho. This stage includes also the capture of Ai, the conclusion of a treaty with the Gibeonites, and the defeat of five Judean kings. From archaeology there is ample evidence concerning the factual character of the account in Joshua, although the destruction of Jericho is, so far, an unexplained matter, since much evidence points to its destruction a century before the arrival of the main body of Hebrews. This would be accounted for if we were to assume that it fell originally to a group of Israelites who entered Palestine before the refugees from Egypt.

The third stage of the Conquest was directed at the northern part of the land. The cities of the Plain of Esdraelon seem to have held out against the invading Israelites, and were not actually in their control until the time of David. The Israelites were more successful against the chief city of the north, Hazor.

As the people settled, most of them locating in the central part of Palestine, they divided the entire land among the tribes. The center of their united life was Shiloh, where there was a shrine sacred to the Lord.

During the next two hundred years Israel was subjected to invasions and border wars, just as the Canaanites had been before them. The Midianites and Ammonites, pressing into the fertile land, brought continual threats. At the same time there was occasional tribal strife among the Israelites themselves.

In this situation a fairly regular pattern developed. Although there was little settled unity among the tribes there would appear in each emergency an individual who possessed some particular qualifications for leadership, and who was able to rally a measure of united support, so that the emergency could be victoriously resolved. These men, and one woman, were known as the judges. They were individuals of heroic mold, who generally disclaimed any personal advantage; rather, after the issue which had called them forth had been decided, they sank back into relative obscurity.

The Philistines, however, were not so satisfactorily overthrown. The biblical story makes it plain that the tribe of Dan was displaced entirely by these invaders. The story of Samson shows how, in spite of the most energetic measures against them, the Philistines were able to bring the Israelites to their knees. This was the situation which prevailed at the opening of the Books of Samuel, about 1000 B.C.

The Meaning of the Story

The Israelites looked back to the Exodus as the outstanding sign of God's grace to them. In the same way they regarded the Conquest as a sign of that grace continued and of God's providential care. Here, too, was powerful confirmation of what had been learned in the Exodus and at Sinai, that God was pre-eminently the God of history, actively moving in the affairs of men and of nations. In his hand were the issues of their lives.

God's control of history is nowhere more evident than in the choice and preparation of the judges. Here were men who were leaders not so much because of their special qualifications, although they undoubtedly had them, but because the Spirit of God came upon them, heightening their natural abilities and making them the representatives of God, the agents of his purpose. These men have been called "charismatic" leaders, the term pointing to their unique position as endowed by the Spirit for their task. They were the sign of God's presence and activity in the affairs of that nation.

In this history, moreover, there is always evident a specialized point of view. The story of the Conquest and of the period of the judges is told so as to bring out the meaning which the people found in their own history. This was the simple truth that as long as they remained the people of the Covenant, united in a common purpose, true to one another and to the God of the Covenant, things went well. When they lived in selfish isolation or in idolatrous denial of the Covenant religion they were humiliated. As at Sinai they had come to meet a God of grace, so in their history they learned that he is also a God of judgment.

The Rise of the Israelite Kingdom

The Setting

A period of about one century covers the time when the Israelite people, heretofore without much central power, were welded into a single, relatively stable kingdom. The same period includes the three great figures of this kingdom, Saul, David, and Solomon.

The situation which gave rise politically to the need for a monarchy has already been sketched. The arrival of the Philistine people and their increasing subjugation of the Israelites was far more serious than the temporary emergencies of the previous two centuries. Against the highly developed civilization of the Philistines and their control of iron the Hebrews under the old tribal system were relatively powerless.

To be considered in the situation facing the Israelites was also a changing pattern in the north. During the time of the judges there had grown up a strong state in the region along the coast in the north, the Phoenicia of the Bible. Although the Phoenicians seem not to have engaged in extensive warfare, the state did grow increasingly influential.

At the same time that this new state was developing, another to the northeast was growing under a new wave of invasions from Arabia. These new peoples were the Arameans, whose aggressive efforts built up a powerful nation with its center at Damascus. This nation, the Aram, or Syria, of the Bible, was one of the strongest opponents to Israel's claims and to her security.

The Story

The story of the rise of the Hebrew kingdom and its spread within three generations is told in the Bible mainly as the story of three men, the three kings of the united kingdom, with some attention paid to another, Samuel, who was influential in the selection of two of them.

The first king, Saul, was in many respects a parallel to the previous judges. The biblical narrative makes plain the fact that he was chosen for his task by God himself. His early exploits are like those of the judges. He first delivered Jabesh-gilead, in Transjordan, from an invasion by the Ammonites. Following this victory he was successful in dislodging the Philistines from the central part of Palestine, but not from Jerusalem nor from the important Plain of Esdraelon.

Saul's successor had been his rival during the closing years of his reign. When David came to power he was able, in a remarkably short time, to create a political unity out of what had hitherto been only loosely organized tribes. His first act of significance was the capture of Jerusalem, which had never been under Israelite control. This city, well situated, and with no sectional loyalty attached to it, was a wise choice for the capital of the growing kingdom. David was also successful in uniting the entire territory and in securing its borders, whether by conquest of neighboring nations or by alliance with them. In his reign the nation prospered economically because of its position on the trade routes of the world, and there developed a stable system of government.

This system was continued and expanded by Solomon, the son and successor to David. Solomon spent his time, and the wealth of the nation, in a vast program of building and government projects, the while neglecting the boundaries of the kingdom. As a result of his shortsighted policies the nation deteriorated. Taxation and forced labor drafts ensured popular resentment; available sources of revenue from the outside fell off; and one by one the limits of the Davidic kingdom were reduced. At Solomon's death the kingdom was ready for dissolution.

The Meaning of the Story

The relation between factual reporting and interpretation of facts in the Bible is nowhere clearer than in the way in which the rise of the Hebrew kingdom is told in the Books of Samuel. Here is history, but not merely the chronicling of certain events or the chronological recital of a nation's career. Rather the events are told in such a way that the faith of the people is clearly expressed.

For example, this story gives expression to the continued conviction that God is the Lord of history. Although it was during the reign of Solomon that worship at the Temple developed in magnificence and influence, the account of the history shows clearly that men come to know God, not so much in the Temple as in the movements of nations and in the affairs of the kingdom. In the complicated developments during the time of Saul, David, and Solomon, and in the relationships of these men and of the nation to kingdoms outside the borders of Israel, one sees the word and will of God.

The biblical narrative also brings out the fact that the kingdom itself was in one sense a departure from the will of God for his people. Samuel, the priest and prophet and seer in one, living at the time of the birth of the kingdom, illustrates the reservations felt about this new government. The one ruler of the nation was God, and the kingdom of Israel was ideally the Kingdom of God, not the kingdom of any earthly monarch. A political kingdom could easily serve to destroy that idea. At the same time the scriptural account indicates that, under the extreme conditions existing at the time, the kingdom could serve a good purpose. If it were to develop in such a way that the king would be the constant representative of God and would rule as for God, then the kingdom would itself be an important means of accomplishing Israel's Covenant responsibility.

This period also saw the rise of the prophets as a force in Israel. It was still some years before the great efforts of Elijah and Elisha in Israel, and more years before the time of the great writing prophets. But here, at this critical juncture of Israel's history, when the balances hung lightly, and when the nation needed the guidance of the Spirit of God, there appeared a new line of spiritual leaders, the first of a long line of individuals who were, in a real sense, Israel's greatest glory.

Nathan, in the reign of David, is an ideal example of these early prophets. Standing before the king, condemning him for his cruelty and unconcern, Nathan is the representative of the people in their native distrust of an increasing central power which was tending toward autocratic tyranny. But more important, he is the representative of the ancient Sinai tradition, which, far from dying out, was coming alive again in this period. In him and his words we hear the Covenant principles enunciated again, not in relation to the old nomadic life of the desert, but in relation to the complexity of Palestinian life in the days of the monarchy. These prophets, the men of the Spirit, were the glory of Israel; they were also the ones through whom the word of God continued to come to the nation, as they pointed out, without reservation or compromise, the meaning of the life of that day and of the political and economic developments of the nations.

With its roots in this period, there shortly arose the concept of an ideal king, a concept which Israel never entirely lost. In each successive ruler the nation saw the possible ideal, and as each successive ruler showed plainly that he was far from ideal, the thought of the people turned again to the ideal, especially to the future ideal, and they looked forward to some decisive act of God whereby the ideal would be made actual.

The Divided Kingdom to the Fall of Israel

The Setting

At the death of Solomon, in 922 B.C., the Israelite kingdom split into two sections, which pursued their more or less independent courses for the next two centuries.

When this period in Israel's history began, Egypt had emerged to new power and had entered the troubled affairs of Palestine again. After the middle of the ninth century, however, it played little part in Palestinian affairs. On the other hand, there was a new power which played a decisive part, the Assyrian nation in a new phase of its life. This nation became a controlling factor in Israel's history for nearly two centuries. As early as the tenth century Assyria had been rising to power, and by the ninth century the might of that nation had been so successfully developed that with powerful blows it was bringing the entire ring of surrounding nations to their knees.

After a short time of comparative quiescence the Assyrian power again revived in the middle of the eighth century under Tiglath-pileser III. Pursuing an energetic policy of warfare, systematic destruction of cities, and depopulation of lands, the new Assyrian rulers were able to control the entire Mediterranean world by the end of the century.

The Story

The death of Solomon found the Israelite kingdom in a desperate situation. It was crippled by heavy taxation, and had lost much of its external revenue. The northern part of the land, always more independent than the south, united under a former officer of the royal court, Jeroboam, to oppose the claims of Solomon's son, Rehoboam. The two divisions of the kingdom drew apart, the north, or Israel, comprising most of the land, and the south, or Judah, covering the city of Jerusalem, the surrounding territory of the tribe of Judah, and the neighboring tribe of Benjamin. In the north, where the rulers made serious attempts to establish the nation as an independent entity, sanctuaries were built to counteract the influence of the Solomonic Temple in Jerusalem.

In the beginning of the ninth century there came, in the north, a change of dynasty and the establishment of the house of Omri, a military leader. He and his son, Ahab, were able to strengthen the land, while Ahab was partly responsible for a coalition of small powers which turned back the Assyrian armies at Karkar in 853 B.C.

The dynasty of Omri was replaced by that of Jehu after an internal rebellion. One of the reasons for the success of this rebellion was submission to Assyria, but the effect was to establish Israel as a prosperous nation. Under Jehu's grandson, Jeroboam II, the nation became economically great, but its greatness was built upon a drastically altered pattern of life and on increasingly corrupt practices in economic and political affairs.

This prosperity had no sooner come to be than it was destroyed. Under a series of blows by the revived power of Assyria the nation of Israel was brought to ruin, the capital city of Samaria destroyed, and the land subjected to the Assyrian policy of colonization whereby the Israelites were scattered in the remote parts of the Assyrian Empire and the cities of Israel settled with foreigners brought in from other conquered lands.

The Meaning of the Story

The period sketched above is treated both in the "historical books" of the Old Testament and in the books of prophecy. In both sources the same view of history is plain, and it is no new thing but a reaffirmation of the ancient truth that the high privilege which the nation enjoyed in its Covenant with God was also a great responsibility. The Covenant, which was a ground of security, was nevertheless not a ground of presumption.

Here, too, is the developing understanding and application of the Covenant principle that the relationship of man to God is not divorced from the relationship of man to man, but that, on the contrary, the latter is the indispensable evidence of the former. The prophets of this period are constantly judging the social, economic, and political life of the nation and people, not merely by ethical standards, but by religious ones.

It was in terms of the quality of its human relationships that the nation was judged. The prophets brought a searching light to bear on marketplace and home, on royal palace and place of business; and in such seemingly inconsequential matters as luxurious fittings, dishonest measures, and senseless amusements, they read the death sentence at the judgment bar of God.

The Exile and Return

The Setting

From the year 612 B.C., which saw the destruction of Nineveh, the capital of Assyria, until 539 B.C., the year of the entry of the Persian general Cyrus into Babylon, the dominant power of the world, so far as the fortunes of the Hebrew people were concerned, was the neo-Babylonian, or Chaldean Empire. The most powerful of its rulers was Nebuchadnezzar, whose rule of over forty years pushed Babylonian power to the borders of Egypt.

Palestine came into the Babylonian Empire, along with the rest of the eastern Mediterranean lands. Judah, including the city of Jerusalem, was regarded as vassal territory. There were two revolts against Babylon. In the first one Nebuchadnezzar captured the Judean king and a number of the leaders of the land, but did not completely destroy the city. In the second revolt the full weight of Babylonian destruction was felt. The city was ruined, the Temple burned, and only a relatively few leading people were left in the land, the rest being carried off to Babylon.

Nebuchadnezzar was succeeded by Nabonidus, whose uncertain policies alienated certain parts of the Empire. His son, Belshazzar, ruled for a time, but a new coalition of power was already taking the center of the stage. This was the Persian Empire, elements of which had been influential in the destruction of Nineveh. In the middle of the sixth century Media was joined to Persia, and in 539 B.C. Cyrus II entered the city of Babylon as its conqueror. Egypt was brought into the Persian Empire in 525 B.C., and in the next fifty years there were two unsuccessful attempts to annex the lands of Greece.

Persian rule, which lasted well over two centuries, was finally brought to an end by the remarkable exploits of Alexander the Great, who in 333 B.C. defeated Darius of Persia, and seized the remnants of his empire.

The Story

Judah, which had survived Assyrian invasions at the end of the eighth century, was embroiled thereafter in the changing affairs of Assyria and Egypt, while internally the nation suffered greatly under the reign of Manasseh. Under Josiah, who came to the throne of Judah in 640 B.C., there was a serious effort at political and religious reformation, at least partly successful. It was short success, for in 608 B.C. Josiah was killed at Megiddo by Necho, Pharaoh of Egypt, who was trying to establish Egyptian power following the break of Assyrian rule. Within a few years the tide had completely turned and the entire land of Palestine was virtually under the control of Babylon.

The two revolts of Jerusalem against Babylonian power, that of 597 B.C. and that of 587-586 B.C., have already been mentioned. At the end of the second the Judean nation, like Israel a century and a quarter before, ceased to exist as a political entity.

A few people were left in the land of Palestine. These were to be governed by Gedaliah, who was appointed by the Babylonians. He was assassinated, and, in dread of Babylonian revenge, the remainder of responsible people departed to Egypt, where they disappeared from the biblical story.

The center of that story now shifts to Babylon. Not much is known from the biblical narrative about the life of the exiles in Babylon. But it is in Babylon, not in Palestine nor in Egypt, that the story eventually began again. The exiles must have lived a generally undisturbed life, although at certain periods they may have seen considerable persecution, and the life of such displaced refugees would not have been easy in any age or situation. They managed to preserve their unity around their faith, and by turning anew to the literature of the Law and the Prophets which they had carried into exile with them, they were able to explore and understand that faith as they had not before. The development of the synagogue as a religious center in this period undoubtedly helped to keep alive and to intensify the characteristic marks of the Hebrew faith. Another development in these years was the creation of extensive religious literature.

With the end of the Babylonian Empire the fortunes of the Jews changed markedly. The Persian monarchs, generally more enlightened than either their Assyrian or Babylonian predecessors, followed a policy of encouraging nationalism and the creation of puppet states, with loyalty to the central Persian power, thus reversing the systematic disruption of national loyalties which had marked previous attempts at world empire.

Under this policy the Jews were encouraged to reconstruct a kind of national existence in Judah. First under Zerubbabel the Temple was rebuilt, then in the middle of the fifth century, Jerusalem was rebuilt with walls. The work of these early pioneers was helped by Nehemiah, a civil leader, and by Ezra, the scribe, who was instrumental in establishing the Law as a central, controlling factor of national life. From this time, down to the spread of the Greek Empire, the fortunes of the Jews continued relatively unchanged.

The Meaning of the Story

The period sketched above is treated both in historical and prophetic books in the Bible. In them we find the truth that God's judgment falls on any nation, even that nation which is peculiarly his own, for its failure to live by his just and righteous demands. No nation is exempt from the judgment of God in history. The other side of the truth, also plain in the Bible, is the unending mercy of God, mercy by which a remnant is saved. In this mercy men may hope, even in the midst of judgment and despair, as they are pointed to the future which is God's and in which his mercy will be fully known.

In this period hope became an increasingly strong element of life and faith. The returnees were themselves literally the creation of hope, as, nurtured on the prophetic hope, they had learned to look to God and to trust in his purpose for the future.

It was also a time of potential Messianic realization. As the men of this restoration period began the work of rebuilding a nation they were, at least potentially, building toward the perfect Kingdom of God on earth. That their efforts did not succeed, and that they failed once again as their ancestors had failed before them, did not destroy the hope of the coming Kingdom, but in fact intensified it.

This period also saw the creation of Judaism as a true religious entity. National ambitions were not ignored, but by and large, the attention of people turned more and more to the spiritual aspects of their life, primarily to the Law as the controlling factor of life, and to the Temple as the center of worship.

The Intertestament Period
(The Maccabees and the Herods)

The Setting of the Story

Another in the long series of crises in the course of Israel's history came when the empire of Alexander the Great, so recently established, broke apart at his death. Among the generals who contended for control of the empire, or parts of it, two were most important for the Jews. Ptolemy Lagi was able to hold Egypt, and Seleucus the territory of Syria and the east. Palestine continued to be, as it had been for much of the time in the past, the scene of conflict between the northeast and the southwest. For over a century Egypt maintained its hold on the land, but always under pressure from Syria. Finally, in 198 B.C., Antiochus III of Syria was able to annex Palestine to the Syrian Empire. From this time on the situation in Judea grew steadily worse.

Alexander himself had been an energetic apostle of Greek culture, and his conquests had strengthened the influence of Greece on the entire world. His successors followed his pattern in the main, but it was in Syria that the most strenuous effort to impose Hellenic (Greek) ideas and customs upon the whole of the kingdom was made. This effort ran in direct opposition to the faith and religious culture of the Jews, and out of the struggle between the two emerged the Maccabean Age and, ultimately, the conquest of Palestine by Rome.

The Story

Antiochus IV was the most ardent of the proponents of Greek culture among the Syrian rulers. He was also the most determined opponent of the Jewish religion which resisted his efforts. When other attempts had been ineffectual he began a policy aimed at systematic destruction of the Jewish religion. In 168 B.C. the Temple in Jerusalem was desecrated and most of the practices of Judaism were declared to be unlawful, punishable by death.

Jewish reaction was at first undecided, some of the Jews being convinced that resistance was impossible or useless. Some capitulated, others went to martyrs' deaths. But eventually revolt crystallized around the family of a priest, Mattathias, who, with his five sons, began to resist the decrees of the king. Judas, one of the sons, nicknamed the Maccabee, or the Hammerer, was the first leader in the revolt which began as guerrilla activity in Judea. The progress of the revolt is set forth in the Books of Maccabees which tell how Jerusalem was recaptured and the Temple cleansed and rededicated in 164 B.C.; how religious freedom was won for the Jews; and how under succeeding leaders of the Maccabean line, a measure of political freedom was finally gained.

At the beginning of the last century B.C. the effort began to fray out. The Maccabean descendants were engaged in internal strife, complicated by a developing antagonism between two parties of the Jews, the Pharisees and the Sadducees. In one particularly critical time an appeal was made to Pompey, the Roman general, who obliged by assuming control of the land for Rome.

An Idumean, Antipater, was declared by Julius Caesar to be procurator of Judea, his place being taken in 40 B.C. by his son, Herod, who was then declared king of the Jews by the Romans. Herod ruled until 4 B.C., and at his death the land was divided, Galilee going to Antipas, the land in the northeast to Philip, and Judea to Archelaus, all sons of Herod. Archelaus was deposed in A.D. 6, and for the next thirty-five years Judea was governed by Roman procurators.

The Meaning of the Story

Since many of the events of this time lie outside the realm of the biblical Canon they are not a part of the history which the people of God remembered as their own and in which they found meaning. There were, however, many important developments in this period which in one way or another touched upon that history.

Not the least of these was the struggle for liberty in the Maccabean revolt. Here was one of the great epochs of all history as a few Jews, against overwhelming odds, resisted the organized pressure of paganism and heathenism. In the stories of the Maccabean martyrs and heroes a staunch and practical faith is given clear expression.

It was in this period that the dominant themes of Judaism were fixed in the form they hold in New Testament times. These themes are stated in the books written and read in this time, many of which survive today in the body of literature known as the Apocrypha and the Pseudepigrapha. Still more are coming to light in the discoveries of literary remains at the Dead Sea.

Prominent among these themes was a pronounced apocalypticism, the conviction that history was drawing to its close, an event which would be catastrophic so far as the heathen nations and the wicked in Israel were concerned, but which would bring the blessings of the divine Kingdom for the faithful.

Another development was an intensified devotion to the Law as a way of life. This was characterized at times by a fanatic concern with minutiae, but in the main it was a serious attempt to apply the general principles of the Old Testament Law to the commonplaces of life in Galilee and Judea of the Roman period.

In the same period there grew increasingly intense suspicions between the major parties in Judaism, the Pharisees and the Sadducees, with divergent views on almost every question, religious and political. Another group, the Zealots, concentrated on the political situation and schemed for freedom from Rome. Finally, there were the Essenes, or Essene-like groups, who, trying to maintain a pure way of life in the midst of encroaching secularism, and finding it increasingly impossible, withdrew to the seclusion of monastic communities where they prepared themselves for the advent of the heavenly Kingdom, or for war with the forces of evil, or for both.

In every way the Maccabean struggle left its mark upon the people, so that freedom from foreign oppression, once tasted, became the dominant dream. Roman occupation of the land, and the harsh realities of everyday life, never easy in Palestine, nourished that dream. Not all the individuals or all the parties of Judaism visualized the future in exactly the same way, but they were all at least turned toward the future as the New Testament era dawned.

New Testament Times (I)

The Setting

Herod, who had been declared king of Judea by Rome in 40 B.C., was an energetic ruler and builder. Among his major projects was the reconstruction of the Temple in Jerusalem, a work which began in 19 B.C. and continued over many years, with the main part of the building completed before the birth of Jesus.

At Herod's death in 4 B.C., under the terms of his will, and with the approval of Rome, his kingdom was divided among his three sons. To Archelaus went the title of king and the territory of Judea and Samaria with part of Idumea; to Herod Antipas went Galilee and Perea; and to Philip went the country east of the Jordan. The last two held control for considerable time, Herod Antipas until A.D. 39 and Philip until A.D. 34, but Archelaus was deposed in A.D. 6 and the territory of Judea and Samaria was placed under Roman procurators, among whom Pontius Pilate appears from A.D. 26 to 36.

Meanwhile a grandson of Herod, Agrippa, had succeeded in winning the favor of Caligula. When Caligula was made emperor of Rome in A.D. 37, Agrippa was declared king of Philip's territory, to which was added that of Antipas in A.D. 39 when Antipas was banished to Gaul for alleged treachery. Finally in A.D. 41 the Emperor Claudius gave to Agrippa all of Judea and Samaria, making his kingdom equal to that of Herod the Great.

In three years Agrippa was dead. Since his son was considered too young to succeed him, the land was again placed under procurators, among whom were Felix (from A.D. 52 to 60) and Festus (from A.D. 60 to 62). Meanwhile resentment of Roman rule had been on the increase, and in the procuratorship of Florus in A.D. 64 to 66 it broke out into open revolution.

Rome was quick to act to suppress such rebellion and by A.D. 67 had stamped out resistance in Galilee and most of Judea. In A.D. 68 the Roman general Vespasian laid siege to the city of Jerusalem. The death of Nero forced Vespasian to return to Rome before the climax of the war had been reached, but in A.D. 70 his son Titus returned to besiege the city. After terrible suffering on the part of the inhabitants the city was captured, the Temple destroyed, and vast numbers of the Jews were carried off as slaves. The intent was to put an end to Jewish resistance forever, but it was not entirely successful. In the period from A.D. 132 to 135 another rebellion broke out under Bar-Cochba. When the Jews were once again defeated, the city of Jerusalem was rebuilt as a Gentile city, renamed Aelia Capitolina, and an edict was proclaimed that no Jew would be permitted to enter it.

In the Palestine of Jesus' day Roman rule was not simply a fact of politics, it was the dominant feature of everyday life. Although Roman policy varied from province to province, and was generally wise and enlightened, there were certain aspects of that rule which made for constant friction and difficulty. One of these was the ever-present army, the actual instrument of administration, with a centurion and his band stationed in the leading towns and cities. Another irritating feature was the system of taxation, so extensive that every item had its tax, as did every operation and activity. Taxes were apportioned to districts in total amounts under a system which made for corruption among the collectors and for hostility in those being taxed.

The twin evils of poverty and slavery went hand in hand in every part of this world. The heavy taxation added to the already difficult pattern of life in Palestine made for economic insecurity. And although the average Jew did not own slaves, he was constantly faced with slavery as a fact and even as a possibility for himself, for most of the open rebellions against Rome ended with the capture of large numbers of Jews as slaves and there was, moreover, always the prospect that debt would drive a person into slavery.

Religion, for the average inhabitant of Palestine, had several centers. Because of the great importance that had been attached to the minute observance of the Law and because of the multiple applications of the Law that had been made to contemporary life, religion was first of all a matter of everyday existence, of the way one lived in home and community, and of the way one conducted his business. Another center was found in the local synagogues which had grown in importance during the two centuries before the birth of Christ. Most towns had synagogues which were centers of learning, worship, and fellowship. Finally, there was the Temple, the great ritual center which drew attention and attracted pilgrimages all through the year, but especially on certain occasions of a man's life and at the times of religious festival.

Greek culture had won a respectable place in Palestine through the Romans who lived there and through the Herodian rulers whose contacts with Rome and need to keep the favor of Rome made them outwardly enthusiastic in their support of things Roman and Grecian. In the New Testament the story has a background of Galilean farming and fishing, of simple homes and of village life among the peasants; or of Jerusalem with the Temple; or of Judean homes. The face of Palestine which the contemporary world would have noticed would have been far different, a face of expensive buildings, of adroit political maneuvering, and of firm Roman power.

The Story

It is in a series of events that took place during the time sketched above that the people of God have come to see the central part of their own story. In the happenings of a few short years during this time they have found the clue to the entire past and the shape of the future; here they have come to understand the great, once-and-for-all act of God by which they are called to be his people and, in fact, *made* to be his people.

For these events relatively few historical sources remain, so that the effort to reconstruct them simply as "history" leaves one very much in the dark. There is much we would like to know and do not know. Outside the Bible there are only a few, isolated references to the fact of Jesus' work and they establish merely the fact that such a person actually lived. When we turn to the Church's own literature we find it concerned primarily with the *meaning* of Jesus' life, teaching, death, and resurrection, and only secondarily concerned with the facts of his day-by-day life or the circumstances under which he lived and ministered.

This reminds the reader of the Gospels that these books are not history books in the commonly accepted sense of the term. The Synoptics (Matthew, Mark, and Luke), as well as John, are not designed to serve as biographies of the man Jesus. When one looks at the amount of material they contain and particularly at the proportionate attention given in these books to certain parts of Jesus' life, he discovers that, at best, the Gospels cover only a few days in connection with Jesus' birth, and have only a fragment concerning his early life. They concentrate on what he said and did during a couple of years or so, but even then give special attention to what he did and suffered in Jerusalem during one week, and how he died and rose from the dead. Such a survey of the Gospels simply confirms the fact that the story they have to tell is not just a "history" but the recital of what God has done and of the way he acted in behalf of his people. This recital is tied in with earthly events but it is not itself just an earthly event.

From the Gospel records we can see some things with relative certainty. They indicate that it is important to know that Jesus was born in extraordinary circumstances. His birth was heralded by angelic announcement. He was born of a virgin of the house and line of David. In spite of these extraordinary circumstances and in spite of early expectation on the part of a few, he seems to have grown up in obscurity. In the early years of his life he probably worked as a carpenter, although it is important that the ones who formed the Gospel tradition and wrote the Gospels did not find it necessary to describe the details of his personal life or of his relations to the members of his family.

All the Gospels agree that the real opening of the ministry of Jesus was the coming of John the Baptist, preaching a baptism of repentance and prophesying the coming of the Messiah. It is probable that the baptism which John preached and which his followers received was meant to be taken as the entrance into the community of the Messiah who was to come.

After Jesus was himself baptized by John he is represented in the Gospels as having undergone an experience in the wilderness which centered on the character of the Messianic office which he was about to undertake. Following this, he began a public ministry in Galilee, particularly in the towns around the Sea of Galilee. This ministry, including preaching both in the synagogues and out of doors, and miracles of healing, attracted a following. Early in his ministry he selected a band of disciples, twelve in number, symbolizing the wholeness of Israel, and sent them out on tours of service like his own.

At the same time that his following was increasing it was perhaps inevitable that opposition should also grow. This opposition centered on Jesus' apparent disregard of the Law, particularly as it related to observance of Sabbath and ceremonial traditions. While this type of opposition was largely confined to the leaders, there were probably opponents of Jesus among the general populace also, in particular those who recognized him as a threat to their normal securities, either economic or social. The Gospels represent Jesus as spending some time, after this early opposition developed, outside the region of Galilee, visiting such places as Tyre, and the Decapolis on the other side of the Jordan.

Following a return to Galilee he began a journey to Jerusalem which he regarded as particularly significant. In the course of the journey, and during a sojourn in the southern region around Jerusalem for an indeterminate period of time, the opposition to him and his ministry crystallized.

The Gospel story continues with that part which is regarded by the writers as especially important, covering a week which began with Jesus' public entrance into Jerusalem in such a way that it became evident that he was presenting himself to the nation as the promised Messiah. His entrance was accompanied by popular acclaim and was followed by his act of symbolic purification of the Temple, an act which was interpreted by his enemies as an intolerable outrage. Jesus was arrested after one of his disciples had turned traitor; and after a hurried trial before the Sanhedrin, the leading court of the Jews, and another before Pontius Pilate, the Roman procurator, he was executed by crucifixion.

The Gospels agree that this was not the end, but that this same Jesus rose from the dead, appearing to various of his disciples for the space of forty days. Following these appearances he was taken up into heaven. Almost immediately, according to the Acts of the Apostles, his disciples began preaching in his name in the city of Jerusalem, and great numbers of people were drawn into a fellowship of believers which was the beginning of the Christian Church.

The Meaning of the Story

The above bare facts of the "life" of Jesus do not constitute the message of the Gospels. Even if they were expanded to take in all the detailed facts extant in the Gospels they would still not constitute the message. The Gospels are the expression of the faith that this One who thus lived, worked, died, and rose, was in a unique way the act of God, that in him God was uniquely present with men, that in him all the purpose of God came to full expression and realization, and that in him and in him alone men are enabled to receive the salvation which God offers to them.

The Gospels do not represent all of the information about Jesus which the Church had at the first stages of its existence. Rather they are a special selection and special arrangement, designed to focus attention on certain truths and certain facts.

One of these is the fact that in Jesus of Nazareth the whole purpose of the past comes to realization, as in him the whole movement of the history of God's people reaches its climax. This is most often expressed in the conviction, basic to all the Gospels, that Jesus is the Messiah, that is, that he stands in special relation to God as his representative, and, at the same time, in special relation to men. He is regarded in the Gospels as the Son of God, fully divine, and no less as the Son of Man in that he combines in his person and his work the gracious purpose of God and the proper response of man. He is seen to be the One in whom the vocation of the Israelite nation is finally fulfilled; he who is the true reflection of God and at the same time the true Servant of God bears in himself all the responsibilities and needs of his brethren.

Another fact that receives strong prominence in the Gospels is the fact that in Jesus the Kingdom of God, or God's rule among men, comes to actualization, so that where Jesus Christ is, there the rule of God has already come to pass. Men are invited by him to enter that Kingdom and, at the same time, in him to discover the power that enables them to live under the rule of God. For, although Jesus proclaimed the Kingdom and issued invitation to enter it, his presentation of the demands of that Kingdom are uncompromisingly absolute, calling for radical decision and complete reversal of life.

This also points to another emphasized meaning in the Gospels, that in Jesus God's will to forgive, his unchangeable love, is brought to perfect expression. The death of Jesus is regarded not as total tragedy, as it would be in any other way of thinking, but as the means whereby alienation between God and man is brought to an end, and the means whereby men receive grace and strength, forgiveness and acceptance. The bond of union between Jesus and the ones who are his is simply faith, a faith which includes acceptance of certain facts but also actual union with the Lord.

Basic to the Gospels, and in fact to the entire New Testament, is the proclamation that Jesus, and he alone, is the Lord of life. To him is due all loyalty and all honor. The Gospels themselves are the expression of the one central faith of the Church, in that they locate in a place, Palestine, and in a definite time, during the procuratorship of Pontius Pilate, One who stands so fully in the place of honor and worship normally reserved for God alone, that there can be no question of his equality with God and of the absolute claims of his Kingdom.

New Testament Times (II)

The Setting of the Story

The historical setting of the close of the New Testament has already been sketched. There remains a necessity to note the changed geographical pattern. The pattern of the Old Testament history has been described as a narrow "S" running along the fertile strip of land from Mesopotamia through Palestine into Egypt. The geographical pattern of the history of the spread of the Christian Church changed radically, in harmony with the different structure of the civilized world and with the energetic newness of the gospel.

In the New Testament the pattern is clearly that of expanding circles, a pattern which the historian of the Acts of the Apostles follows as he traces the expansion of Christianity from its beginning in Jerusalem, through Judea and Samaria, and finally "to the end of the earth," as the gospel comes with its foremost advocate, the Apostle Paul, to the city of Rome.

The world of the New Testament is the world of the Roman Empire, with its great centers of government, culture, and commerce. It was a world which radiated not from Jerusalem but from Rome. In turn, the roads of the empire brought all the world, its produce and its tax, to Rome. In the first century A.D. it was a glamorous world, cultured, cosmopolitan, and wealthy, at least so far as the leaders were concerned.

One of the primary marks of this world was its attention to new religions, accelerated by a decaying paganism and by a reaction against excessive immorality. Judaism itself was attracting adherents by its high moral code, and the secret cults from the East were winning others who were searching for assurance of salvation and cleansing.

The Story

The Book of the Acts opens with Pentecost, when the world-wide character of the Christian faith was evidenced and the Church defined as a missionary enterprise. Pentecost, taking place some fifty days after the Crucifixion, marked the gift of the Holy Spirit to the small group of disciples, who thus received the power and courage to initiate the divine commission. What they actually began to proclaim in Jerusalem is clearly indicated in the Book of the Acts, and elsewhere in the New Testament, for it remains as a constant feature of the entire literature: that in Jesus Christ the New Age, the age of God's purpose, has dawned; that this age is marked by God's power in peculiar measure and by the direct gift of his Spirit; that the age is moving to its conclusion when the Lord Jesus will return; and that meanwhile redemption is offered to all who name the name of Jesus as Lord.

A community of the faithful began to form quickly in Jerusalem, with certain distinctive practices, although it also incorporated some of the normal features of Judaism. In worship and in life the believers gave witness to the Lord, to his love, to his death, to his resurrection, and to his coming again. From the beginning it is probable that members were drawn primarily from the strict

Jews of Palestine, although shortly there appears another group in the Church, the "Hellenists," who were for one reason or another less involved with the narrow orthodoxy of Judaism. Some of these, in their preaching, so sharply attacked contemporary Judaism that persecution broke out. Among those driven out of Jerusalem by the persecution, following the death of Stephen, must have been those who were already disposed to a wider proclamation of the faith, and, as a consequence, we find workers in Samaria and at Antioch. Meanwhile, under the leadership of Peter, the Gentile Cornelius was received into the membership of the Church.

At Antioch the next stage was prepared as the Church there increasingly followed out the implications of a gospel for all the world. It was here, too, that the figure of Paul entered in full prominence.

Paul had been born "Saul" to a Jewish family in Tarsus of Cilicia, which lies in southeastern Asia Minor. At some time Roman citizenship had been bestowed on his family, so that he was born with the rights of a Roman citizen. As a young man he studied in Jerusalem under Gamaliel (mentioned in the New Testament, Acts 5:34-39 and 22:3) at the very time that the Christian faith was gathering force among the Jews. Paul allied himself with those who saw in the movement only a threat to Judaism. In his efforts to stamp it out he started a journey to Damascus where believers were particularly active, but on the way was himself converted by an appearance of the Risen Christ who identified himself with the Church which Paul was persecuting. Blinded for a time, Paul was cured in Damascus through a disciple commissioned by God, and there he was baptized.

After a sojourn in "Arabia" he returned to Damascus and from there came back to Jerusalem for a short visit, which he was compelled to end because of Jewish antagonism. For the next few years he preached in Cilicia and Syria, returning to Antioch when summoned by Barnabas to assist in the work of the Church there.

It was in keeping with the vigorous character of the Church at Antioch that there the decision was made for a wider outreach. Paul and Barnabas were designated as missionaries, setting out on a journey that carried them across the island of Cyprus into Pamphylia. On the journey they preached in the synagogues the kind of sermons illustrated in Acts 13.

When the missionaries returned to Antioch the issue was raised concerning Paul's acceptance of Gentiles into the Christian faith without first requiring acceptance of Jewish rites and laws. A council was held in Jerusalem, resulting in general approval of Paul's policy, although certain minimum requirements were advised.

A second journey was undertaken by Paul shortly afterward, this time with a new companion, Silas. The missioners journeyed through the cities of South Galatia which had been visited before, and then through Asia Minor to Troas, where, in response to a vision, the party sailed for Macedonia. The Book of the Acts mentions the leading cities visited by Paul during his stay in Greece. From here he returned, possibly to Jerusalem for a short visit, then to Antioch.

A third journey carried him once again through Asia Minor, this time to Ephesus, where he stayed two years, concentrating on the Gentiles and working throughout the province of Asia. From here he started a journey to Jerusalem with the purpose of reaching Rome ultimately. Arriving in Jerusalem he was arrested, following a riot in the Temple. For two years he was imprisoned at Caesarea under the Roman governor, Felix. When Festus was made governor he determined to bring Paul to trial at Jerusalem, but Paul appealed to Caesar, as was his right as a Roman citizen.

The last historical record of Paul's life, in the closing chapters of Acts, covers the voyage to Rome, a trip which included a shipwreck and a stay on the island of Malta. On his arrival in Rome he was imprisoned awaiting trial. Here the Book of the Acts closes. The rest of the life of Paul must be reconstructed on the basis of scattered references in his writings and from tradition. Even here there is difficulty. It is fairly certain that he remained a prisoner for two years. If the Pastoral Letters (called Epistles in the King James Version) are from his hand, then it is apparent that he was released and probably fulfilled his ambition to preach in Spain. The most ancient tradition has it that this was the case, and that he was later arrested following the great fire in Rome, and executed by order of Nero in A.D. 67 or 68.

The New Testament does not carry its historical record any further than the arrival of Paul in Rome. Having reached the hub of empire the faith is now preached "to the end of the earth" (see Acts 1:8). This is the end of the story in the sense that everything has been said that needs to be said, and the only thing that remains is the coming of the Lord. Whether the intervening time is short or long is of no great importance.

From the character of certain of the later New Testament writings, however, we can be certain that, following A.D. 64, for the three decades until the end of the century, the situation for the Christian Church steadily worsened so far as relations to the empire were concerned. At the same time it is evident that the Church grew and consolidated its hold on large parts of the empire, as it developed a strong internal organization.

The Meaning of the Story

The influence of Paul on the actual spread of Christianity cannot be overestimated. It is equally impossible to exaggerate the effect of his thought on the culture of the West. He may, in fact, be called the first Western man, in that he gathered together the various streams of influence that have since gone to make up life in the Western world—Jewish, Christian, Roman, and Greek.

His importance for the history of God's people is, of course, in a far different dimension. As with other individuals in this one story, his life is important as an instrument for the purpose of God.

Of still greater importance is his thought, as he worked out and stated the major implications of the gospel. To him and his letters we are indebted for the central doctrines of the Christian faith, especially the oneness of the Body of Christ which is the Church, the character of the Christian life as a life in Christ, the meaning of faith as a way of life in relationship to God through Jesus Christ, and the freedom which is the sure mark of those who are bound by faith and love and hope into the family of God.

THE MESSAGE OF THE BIBLE

The message of the Bible is God's story given through the history of a particular people, whereby he confronts us with himself and his will for our lives. It centers in what he has done, is doing, and will do for us men and for our salvation through Jesus Christ. The Apostles began to preach this good news of God's mighty acts at Pentecost. We begin our study with this preaching which unites the two Testaments as it focuses upon Jesus' own preaching, person, and work.

The Early Preaching of the Apostles

The primary sources for the statements made about the apostolic preaching are Acts 1-10 and passages from the letters of Paul. To be sure, no one of these passages contains a complete sermon, but we have every reason to believe that together they represent accurately the main emphases of the Apostles' proclamation. The passages cited from the letters of Paul indicate the heart of the message which Paul had received from those who had preached the gospel before him. A part of what Paul had received may be seen very clearly in I Corinthians 15:3-7:

> For I delivered to you as of first importance what I also received, that Christ died for our sins in accordance with the scriptures, that he was buried, that he was raised on the third day in accordance with the scriptures . . .

The apostolic preaching may be summarized as follows:

1. *Prophecy has been fulfilled, and the New Age has begun* (Acts 2:14-21, 25-36; 3:17-26; 8:26-40; 10:43; Rom. 1:2). In order to interpret what had taken place in Jesus, these early preachers appealed to their sacred Scriptures, which constitute our Old Testament. They recognized that the Scriptures pointed beyond themselves for their fulfillment and ultimate meaning to a New Age, and they saw the coming of that New Age in Jesus (Gal. 1:4; I Cor. 2:6-8). What God had said through the prophets of old and what he had done among them in Jesus, were tied together in one saving purpose.

2. *God has brought in the New Age through Jesus of Naza-*

reth, *the Messiah of the line of David and the Servant of the Lord*
(Acts 2:36; 3:13; Rom. 1:3-4; Phil. 2:5-11). The words "Messiah" and "Christ" are synonyms meaning "anointed" or "anointed
One." Kings and priests in Israel were anointed for their vocations
(Lev. 6:22; I Sam. 24:6; II Sam. 23:1). Jesus was acclaimed by
the Apostles as the Anointed One in whom Messianic prophecy
was fulfilled. On account of the frequent association of this title
with the name Jesus, the title soon became a part of the name—
Jesus Christ. To speak of him as "descended from David" was to
emphasize his Messiahship, since the Messianic hope was associated with the house of David. The Apostles identified Jesus also
with the Servant of the Lord (Isa. 52:13—53:12) in his suffering
and death, and in his resurrection and exaltation.

3. Jesus *"went about doing good and healing all that were oppressed by the devil"* (Acts 10:38; compare 2:22; 3:6). This quotation from Peter's sermon to Cornelius indicates that the ministry
of Jesus had a part in the earliest apostolic preaching. Jesus'
mighty works were evidence that the Kingdom of God was present
in him (Luke 11:20). His ministry was a part of his saving work,
and without it his death would have been the death of an unknown.

4. He *"was crucified, dead, and buried"* (Acts 2:22-36; 4:10-
12; 7:52; 10:39; Gal. 1:4; I Cor. 1:23; 2:2, 8; 15:3-4; Rom. 4:25;
8:32; Phil. 2:5-8). The crucifixion of Jesus was a part of God's
plan of salvation; yet those who put Jesus to death were guilty of
murder (Acts 2:22-23). According to Galatians 1:4 Jesus "gave
himself for our sins to deliver us from the present evil age." This
is the proclamation of the Atonement in a nutshell. It was Jesus'
purpose in dying to set us free from our sins and transfer us from
the Old Age characterized by all sorts of evil into the New Age of
new life. The Lord's Supper as Paul received it (I Cor. 11:23-26)
is, among other things, a proclamation of "the Lord's death."

5. *Jesus was raised from the dead and is exalted as the Messiah, the Son of God, and Lord of all* (Acts 2:22-36; 3:15; 4:2,
10-12; 5:30-32; 10:36, 40; I Thess. 1:10; I Cor. 15:4-11; Rom.
1:4; 4:25; 8:34; 10:9; Phil. 2:9-11). Jesus had recognized himself as the Messiah (Mark 14:61-62), though he had purified and
enriched the meaning of the term, but it was the Resurrection
above all else that validated his Messiahship for the early disciples. They had recognized Jesus as their Master (Lord) in the
days of his flesh, but it was the Resurrection that gave him the
title "Lord" in its most exalted sense. "Jesus is Lord" may have

been the earliest creed of the Church (see Rom. 10:9; I Cor. 12:3). On account of the association of the word "Lord" with God in the Old Testament and through its association with the resurrection of Jesus, it was charged with the meaning of deity when applied to Christ.

There is no doubt that the Apostles accepted the humanity of Jesus. His death made that clear, and Peter calls him "a man" (Acts 2:22). But the Apostles also accepted him as the Son of God. The expression "Son of God" has a long history. The nation Israel had been known as God's son (Hosea 11:1). This was also true of Israel's king (II Sam. 7:14; Ps. 2:7), for the king was a representative of God before the people and of the people before God. But the king of Israel was not thought of as being divine. In some cases in the New Testament where the expression "Son of God" is used with reference to Jesus, it may designate him as the Messiah of the Kingdom of God, but in most it describes him as the uniquely divine Son of God. It is probable that these two meanings often converge.

6. *Jesus Christ will come again as Judge and Savior to consummate the Messianic Age* (Acts 3:20-21; 10:42; I Thess. 1:10; I Cor. 4:5; 11:26). The New Age had already dawned but it had not yet been brought to its climax. God will consummate his purpose of redemption through the One who has already been crucified and raised from the dead. In the Lord's Supper believers together "proclaim the Lord's death until he comes."

7. *In view of what God has done in Christ and what you have done to Christ, "Repent, and be baptized every one of you in the name of Jesus Christ for the forgiveness of your sins; and you shall receive the gift of the Holy Spirit"* (Acts 2:38; see also 3:19; 5:30-32; 8:26-40; 10:43-48; Rom. 4:25). Peter at Pentecost calls upon his hearers to change their minds and reorient their lives. They had rejected Jesus as their Messiah and were guilty of his death. They were now called upon to accept him as Lord and Christ. Such repentance necessarily includes faith; indeed, it is a turning from sin in commitment to Christ. Repentance, faith, and baptism are all associated with the forgiveness of sins. Baptism marked a person as Christ's and as a member of Christ's people. It meant that a person took a stand and gave to all a witness of his commitment. The gift of the Holy Spirit was associated with baptism but the gift did not always coincide with the act of water baptism (Acts 10:44-48). The gift of the Spirit was a gift of dy-

namic power. His coming was a fulfillment of prophecy (Acts 2:16-21) and of the purpose of both the Father and the resurrected Jesus.

This early preaching of the Apostles was based on the fact of Jesus and the preaching of Jesus, and was in a sense the basis of the books of the New Testament. A comparison of the Apostles' preaching with Jesus' preaching is most illuminating. According to Mark 1:14-15, "Jesus came . . . preaching . . . , and saying, 'The time is fulfilled, and the kingdom of God is at hand; repent, and believe in the gospel.' " We may diagram the comparison like this:

Jesus' Preaching	*The Apostles' Preaching*
(1) The time is fulfilled	(1) Prophecy is fulfilled
(2) The Kingdom of God is at hand	(2) The New Age has begun in Jesus Christ (including all that was said about him above)
(3) Repent and believe in the gospel	(3) Repent, believe, be baptized, and receive the Holy Spirit

Points one and three need no explanation; point two is not so clear. To say the Kingdom of God is at hand is to say that the New Age is dawning. The kingly rule of God came in the Messiah of the Kingdom who lived a life of service, died, and was raised from the dead. The Kingdom is embodied in the King and will be consummated through him.

Israel's Early Rehearsals of God's Mighty Acts

Just as God's mighty acts in Christ are the heart of apostolic preaching and the New Testament, so his mighty acts in Israel are at the heart of the Old Testament. We have seen in the early preaching how God promised the New Age through the prophets, delivered up Jesus to be crucified, raised him from the dead, exalted him to his right hand, and made him Lord and Christ (Acts 2:36).

In order to see clearly the relation between what has already been said and what is about to follow, Acts 13:16-43 should be read. These verses are a summary of Paul's sermon in the synagogue at Antioch of Pisidia. In them Paul makes some of the same emphases found in the earliest preaching. But before Paul makes these distinctly Christian emphases, he recounts some of the mighty acts of God in behalf of ancient Israel: (1) he chose (elected) the patriarchs; (2) made the people great in Egypt; (3) delivered them at the Exodus; (4) bore with them in the wilderness; (5) destroyed the nations in Canaan and gave Israel their inheritance; (6) raised up judges until Samuel the prophet; (7) gave them Saul and later David as king; and (8) of David's posterity he brought Israel a Savior, Jesus, as he promised. In this way Paul shows the unity in the redemptive activity of the one true God.

Deuteronomy 26:5-11 is thought by some to contain Israel's oldest confession of faith. It appears in the ritual for offering the first fruits of the ground. Note the emphasis upon God's deliverance of his people at the Exodus and his gift of the land of Canaan to them:

> "And you shall make response before the LORD your God, 'A wandering Aramean was my father; and he went down into Egypt and sojourned there, few in number; and there he became a nation, great, mighty, and populous. And the Egyptians treated us harshly, and afflicted us, and laid upon us hard bondage. Then we cried to the LORD the God of our fathers, and the LORD heard our voice, and saw our affliction, our toil, and our oppression; and the LORD brought us out of Egypt with a mighty hand and an outstretched arm, with great terror, with signs and wonders; and he brought us into this place and gave us this land, a land flowing with milk and honey' " (Deut. 26:5-9).

Another brief rehearsal of God's mighty acts in behalf of his people Israel is found in Deuteronomy 6:20-25. It is an answer to be made by an Israelite father to his son when the son asks, "What is the meaning of the testimonies and the statutes and the ordinances which the LORD our God has commanded you?" The answer is not abstract but very concrete, centering in the plagues against the Egyptians, the Exodus from Egypt, and the gift of the land of Canaan. Here the Law is rooted in gratitude for the saving acts of God in behalf of his people.

On the occasion of making a covenant at Shechem (Joshua 24) Joshua recites the mighty acts of God in some detail from the selection of Abraham to the gift of the land of Canaan. Many of the elements found in this recital are the same as those enumerated in

Paul's sermon in Acts 13. In fact, there is great similarity among the four passages which have been mentioned. The mighty acts of God recorded in these passages from Deuteronomy and Joshua constitute the skeleton of the first six books of the Old Testament.

In Psalm 78 the recital of what God has done is carried through the choice (selection) of David. In Acts 13, Paul brought the story of God's mighty acts in Israel down to David and then moved immediately to Jesus, who was from David's posterity. Many of the Psalms are proclamations of what God has done and will do (see Pss. 66, 68, 77, 80, 89, 98, 105, 106, 107, 114, 136).

In a sense the whole Old Testament is based on the early proclamation of what God has done for Israel, as that proclamation centers in the Exodus from Egypt. The prophets appeal to the Exodus as they announce the judgment and mercy of God in their day. The Old Testament thought moves on to a new Exodus, a new Covenant, a new entrance of the land, and a new David.

Though the earliest confessions of Israel's faith (Deut. 26:5-11; 6:20-25; Joshua 24) do not mention creation, the time came when creation constituted a very important part of Israel's confession of faith: "Our help is in the name of the LORD, who made heaven and earth" (Ps. 124:8). Creation was a part of the story of salvation itself. The manifestation of God's sovereignty in creation is a ground for faith in his ability to save at any time. All of God's mighty acts in the past bring assurance of the reality, love, and power of God for his people in every situation. Furthermore, by what God has done, his people are assured that he will fulfill his purpose in the future.

The Story of Salvation

We have already seen how in the early apostolic preaching and in the early Old Testament confessions of faith emphasis was placed upon God's mighty acts of salvation. The Bible as a whole is unified about the activity of the one true God and man's response to his saving work. We are here concerned with the overall story to which the Bible as it now stands bears witness.

It is the story of this salvation that the Bible tells. This story has often been outlined, diagramed, and told. Diagrams similar to the following have proved helpful to many.

This is the movement of the history of salvation in the Bible. This outline emphasizes God's mighty acts of salvation, all of

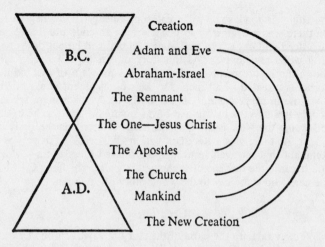

Creation
Adam and Eve
Abraham-Israel
The Remnant
The One—Jesus Christ
The Apostles
The Church
Mankind
The New Creation

which focus in Christ. Jesus Christ is the central point of biblical history and of the Christian's personal history. The Christian moves backward from Christ to creation and forward from Christ to the New Creation, as he stands at the crossroads of history in Christ. He also follows the story from creation to Christ and from Christ to the New Creation. The hourglass begins at the broad base of creation and moves in ever-narrowing fashion to the human family, a part of creation; to the Chosen People; to the Remnant; and on to the One, in whom the purpose of God is fulfilled. Out from the One the hourglass moves in ever-expanding fashion to the Apostles, to the Church as the New Israel, to mankind, and finally to the broad base of the New Creation.

Probably the one word that helps us best to grasp the one story is the word "election." This word, as it is used here, refers to God's choice of the instruments of his purpose. Christ is the unique, elected instrument of God's saving purpose (I Peter 2:4, 6). God chose instruments in the historical movement toward Christ: Abraham, Israel, the Remnant—and instruments in the historical movement toward the consummation of the Kingdom: the Apostles and the Church. He chose specific individuals as well. Even creation itself is a matter of God's election (choice).

The correspondences between the events B.C. and the events A.D. are not accidental. As God created in the beginning and his creation was good, so he will create a new heaven and a new earth. As there was a beginning so will there be an end; and it will not be a dead end but a new beginning. All evil will be put down and God will reign forever. As the story of Adam and Eve clearly shows the involvement of all men in the problem of evil, so the gospel is directed to all men, for their predicament is essentially the same in every generation. As God called into being a special people Israel as the instrument of his saving purpose, so he called into being the New Israel (the Christian Church) as the Body of Christ. As there was a Remnant within Old Israel, so there was a Remnant that received Jesus as the promised Messiah and Savior and became the nucleus of the expanding Church. Jesus Christ is the One who is the key to the whole story of salvation.

Creation

We now take up the parts of the story of salvation one by one. First, we look at God's activity as Creator, especially as this activity is presented in Genesis 1 and 2. It is rather widely accepted that the account of creation found in Genesis 2:4b-25 reached its final form earlier than the account found in Genesis 1:1—2:4a, but the latter passage is surely the right beginning for the biblical narrative. Both of these accounts are written in the thought forms of the ancient Semitic world, though Genesis 2:4b-25 is the more anthropomorphic (that is, speaking of God as if he were a man). Neither of the passages was written to make the modern study of geology, biology, and botany unnecessary; both were written as confessions of Israel's faith in God as Creator.

Genesis 1:1—2:4a was written to say: God is the sovereign Creator whose word is a deed; he created heaven and earth and all that is in them; his creation is orderly and good; he created man in his own image; male and female he created them; he commanded his creatures to multiply and provided for their needs; and he rooted the Sabbath in creation. We may think of Psalm 8 as Genesis 1 set to music. God reveals himself through what he does; his word and work are one (Ps. 33:4). "Heaven and earth" is the Hebrew way of saying "all there is." Creation is good in the sense that it corresponds to God's intention—it is what he ordered.

The image of God in man has been variously defined. It means that man has a likeness to God which no other creature in this world has, and that there is an interpersonal relationship between

God and man. Man is the undersovereign of the sovereign God. He is king over a kingdom for which he is responsible to God. God said to man: ". . . have dominion over the fish of the sea and over the birds of the air and over every living thing that moves upon the earth" (Gen. 1:28). For his stewardship man is responsible to God. God did not make man only male or only female but male and female. Implicit in this fact is the family nature of human life.

Genesis 2:4b-25 makes clear that man is related to the earth; that he is a living being (soul); that he was made to have close relationship with God; that work is a blessing; and that marriage was instituted by God. The fact that the order of creation in Genesis 2:4b-25 differs from the order found in Genesis 1:1—2:4a is inconsequential. The man who put these two stories side by side could see this difference as well as we. It is not the purpose of these passages to debate the chronology or methodology of God's creation, but to state God's relation to the world and to man. In relating man to the earth the author of Genesis 2:4b-25 indicates man's weakness and utter dependence on God for his very existence. Man is not said to have a soul but to become a living soul. The word "soul" has many different meanings in both Testaments, but it usually stresses the nature of man as a unitary being who thinks, feels, and wills. That God and man should be at one is especially clear when Genesis 2 and 3 are read together. To this fact the Scriptures as a whole bear witness.

The Book of Job contains a long section (chs. 38-41) which emphasizes God's creative activity in the beginning and continuously. In connection with these chapters we can place the words of the Psalmist:

> The heavens are telling the glory of God;
> and the firmament proclaims his handiwork (Ps. 19:1).

The heavens do reveal the glory of God but they do not reveal his will. Furthermore, they reveal his glory only to those who believe in him. The heavens said something quite different to a devout Israelite from what they said to a worshiper of the sun, moon, and stars. God may use the study of astronomy to tell a believer something of his glory, but the study of astronomy is not a substitute for the special revelation of God through the Bible.

In some parts of the Old Testament creation is mentioned little or not at all. Salvation is the much more dominant theme. But this does not mean that creation is an unimportant subject. Rather does it mean that God has chosen to reveal himself and his will primarily through a particular history as that history is interpreted by chosen men. God who rules in the affairs of men is the Ruler of the universe. His creative work continues in his control of nature and history. The expressions used to designate God's creation of the world and of man are sometimes used to designate his redemptive work; as for example: "Create in me a clean heart, O God" (Ps. 51:10), and, "I create new heavens and a new earth" (Isa. 65:17).

In Isaiah 40-66 there are brought together strong emphases upon creation, monotheism, salvation, and missions. The emphasis on creation in the Bible is often a missionary emphasis, because it shows God's redemptive concern for all men (see Gen. 1-11).

In Jeremiah 18:11 and Isaiah 45:7 God presents himself as the Creator of evil; this does not mean that he is the Author of sin, but that he brings judgments of condemnation upon sinful men and nations in the process of history.

When God created the world, wisdom was with him (Prov. 8:22-31). In the New Testament we find that Christ is the wisdom of God (I Cor. 1:24, 30); the agent in creation (Col. 1:16; John 1:3, 10); the One in whom all things hold together (Col. 1:17); and the One for whom all things were created (Col. 1:16). The Savior of men is the Creator of men and the Creator of the world in which they live. It is no small matter to confess, "I believe in God the Father Almighty, Maker of heaven and earth."

Adam and Eve

As we move down the hourglass of the story of salvation, we do not move far until we learn that we are not only creatures made in God's image but are also suffering and dying sinners standing in need of a salvation we ourselves cannot provide. Genesis 3 is one of the most profound understandings of the human predicament ever penned. It is the story of the first man and woman and the story of every man and every woman. The word "Adam" is simply a transliteration of a Hebrew word for "man," and "Eve" is a rendering of a Hebrew word for "life" or "living." The understanding that Adam refers to the first man and to every man is altogether in harmony with Hebrew psychology, in which the person and the group often merge.

The third chapter of Genesis says: temptation is a subtle appeal through natural desires (which are basically good) to go beyond limits set by God; sin is seeking to be one's own God, and at the same time it is a family affair; through sin all of life is cursed; and yet God is gracious to rebellious man.

Adam and Eve wanted to be "like God, knowing good and evil." They wanted to determine right and wrong for themselves. They wanted to be independent of God's sovereignty; that is, they wanted an absolute sovereignty of their own—not a freedom within law, but a license without limit. In other words, they wanted to be God. But this story is our story. We are all rebels against God. We are guilty of pride and idolatry. We have worshiped the creature rather than the Creator (Rom. 1:23). We have all gone astray and fallen short of the glory of God. We are sinners born of sinners.

The theme of human sin is continued in Genesis 4-11 in the stories of Cain and Abel, the Flood, and the Tower of Babel. Cain murdered Abel, his brother. In the days of Noah every imagination of man's heart was only evil continually. The builders of the Tower of Babel sought to build a city without God and thereby in pride to make a name for themselves.

Just as the theme of human sin runs through the stories of Cain and Abel, the Flood, and the Tower of Babel, so there runs through these stories the theme of God's judgment upon sin. As Adam is expelled from the garden, Cain is expelled from his people. As death is decreed for Adam, the wicked die in the Flood. As Adam and Eve are estranged the one from the other, the builders of Babel are scattered abroad. Sin issues in further sin, in suffering, and in death.

This suffering may take the form of civil war within, psychosomatic illness, deterioration of personality, the loss of joy, and the hardening of the heart against the will of God (see especially Pss. 32 and 51). It may take many forms in relation to nations or other groups. The prophets never cease to bring Israel before the judgment bar of God for her sin, and God's judgment involves all the horrors of war, famine, pestilence, and captivity.

Genesis 3 makes it clear that there is a connection between sin and death (compare Ezek. 18; Pss. 41, 107). Death, as man experiences it, is what it is because man has sinned. "The sting of death is sin" (I Cor. 15:56). Death in its deepest dimension is not the opposite of biological life but of eternal life (Eph. 2:1, 5; Col. 2:13; Rev. 3:1).

Although Genesis 3 has much to say about temptation, sin, and judgment, we must not overlook what it says about grace: "And the LORD God made for Adam and for his wife garments of skins, and clothed them" (Gen. 3:21). This they did not deserve. This note of the undeserved favor of God runs through the stories of Cain and Abel, the Flood, and the Tower of Babel. Though Cain was driven from his home, God placed his mark of protection upon him. Though destruction by the Flood was terrible, man was given a new chance in Noah. Though men were dispersed in their self-exaltation at Babel, God brought Abraham onto the scene of man's need and gave him the promise of blessing. The story of salvation through a particular community begins with Abraham, and the answer to Babel is eventually given at Pentecost (Acts 2).

Abraham-Israel

The records concerning the patriarchs and Israel set forth God's election of and covenant with a particular people. In other words, the hourglass narrows to the Chosen People. The patriarchal narratives, recorded as we have them after Israel became a nation, are best understood as reflecting Israel's faith. Israel saw parallels between her own history and the history of her forefathers. The patriarchal narratives root Israel's origins in the past and tell us of God's gracious acts in behalf of his Chosen People and in behalf of all men. Further, they give us a candid picture of the response of God's people to him.

God Chooses the Patriarchs

God called Abraham to leave country, kindred, and home to go to a land yet to be designated. God promised to make of him a great nation, to bless him, to make his name great, and to make him a blessing. This promise ends with the famous words, ". . . and in you all the families of the earth will be blessed" (Gen. 12:3, marginal reading). The promise of the land of Canaan was made specifically a little later. When God called Abraham to go, he went. This response is evidence of his faith (Heb. 11:8).

In Genesis 15 God promises Abraham an heir and through that heir a multitude of descendants. "And he believed the LORD; and he reckoned it to him as righteousness" (Gen. 15:6). "Righteousness" here means being right with God. This relation with God is based on Abraham's trust in him, and Paul employs this passage in developing his doctrine of justification by faith (Rom. 4:1-25; Gal. 3:6-9; compare James 2:23). God makes a covenant with Abraham (Gen. 15:7-21) centering in the gift of the land of Canaan to his descendants (vss. 18-21), and God binds himself to Abraham and his descendants without requiring a pledge from Abraham. He initiates the Covenant, and its fulfillment ultimately depends on him. In spite of the fact that Abraham has accepted God's promise of an heir, under the influence of Sarah's suggestion he expresses lack of faith by seeking to have the heir by Sarah's maid, since Sarah is barren.

The account of God's making a covenant with Abraham recorded in chapter 17 tells of the changing of the name Abram to Abraham. This time the Covenant is two-way, for Abraham and his descendants are to bind themselves to God by circumcision. When God promises to Abraham a child by Sarah, Abraham laughs, because both he and Sarah are very old. Later in the narrative Sarah also laughs. In other words, both faith and lack of faith played their part in the life of Abraham. This was Israel's understanding also of her own relationship with God.

One of the most beautifully told and deeply moving stories in all Holy Writ is the story of how God tested Abraham. In the ancient world child sacrifice was a well-established practice. In such a context Abraham was called to sacrifice his only son Isaac, the child of promise. Abraham seems to have responded at a depth of faith he had not known before. He obeyed without murmur, and God taught him that he did not approve of child sacrifice but wanted his son dedicated alive. Abraham's surrender was complete. It is no wonder his name has become almost synonymous with faith. At least some in Israel learned the meaning of this kind of faith. To trust God to fulfill his promise when the very instrument of the promise is about to be destroyed, is the kind of faith that accepts God as the only ultimate security. No longer did Abraham seek to snatch providence from the hands of God and seek to fulfill the promise himself. In the Old Testament, in the New Testament, and through all subsequent generations, men have praised the God of Abraham.

Isaac is a connecting link between Abraham and Jacob, as bearer of the Covenant. The election of Jacob as channel of the Covenant clearly did not rest on Jacob's character. He bargained for his brother Esau's birthright, stole the blessing from his blind father Isaac, attempted to bargain with God at Bethel, and tricked

his father-in-law Laban. No doubt faith played a part in his relation to God, especially at Bethel and Peniel, yet the election and
Covenant were from God and not from Jacob. They were a matter
of grace, not desert (see Gen. 32:10).

The story of Joseph is too well known to be repeated here. Its
unity is more obvious than that of the story of Abraham or Jacob. The conflict between sin and faith is found not in Joseph but
in his brothers, the sons of Jacob (Israel). Joseph is the one
whom God has chosen to be his instrument in saving alive the
Covenant family and others in a time of famine. Joseph's brothers intended evil against him in selling him into slavery, but God
meant it for good (Gen. 50:20). Again it is affirmed that the
Covenant promise is rooted in the sovereign grace of God. God
was working out his purpose of salvation through the patriarchs.

God Delivers and Establishes His People

As we look at the hourglass diagram of the salvation story, we
are reminded that God's election moves to Israel. For not all of
Abraham's or Isaac's descendants were to be the special instrument of his saving purpose. At the same time this does not mean
that God had no purpose for others or was unconcerned about
them (Gen. 16:7-16).

God revealed his election of Israel through the Exodus events
(Ezek. 20:5-6). Some of the early rehearsals of God's mighty
acts as they center in the Exodus from Egypt have already been
noted. The prophets and psalmists also bear witness to the Exodus
redemption (for example, Amos 9:7; Hosea 2:14-15; 11:1; Micah
6:4; Jer. 2:2-7; Pss. 66:6; 78:13; 114:1-8).

At the burning bush God called Moses to be the instrument of
redeeming his people from slavery and revealed to him his name
(Yahweh, the LORD). Eventually the children of Israel crossed the
Red Sea (Hebrew, Reed Sea) as on dry land, and sang with Miriam the song of God's mighty act in behalf of Israel:

> "Sing to the LORD, for he has triumphed gloriously;
> the horse and his rider he has thrown into the sea"
>
> (Exod. 15:21).

Passover became in Israel the festival which commemorated the
Exodus events. God's redemption of his people at the Exodus
serves as a pivot of the theme of redemption throughout the Bible.
He redeems from all sorts of evils: suffering, sin, and death. The

Exodus, Passover, Calvary, and the Lord's Supper are all united for us by Paul in I Corinthians 5:7: "For Christ, our paschal lamb, has been sacrificed."

In spite of God's deliverance of his people from Egyptian bondage, they complained about lack of food and water in the wilderness. God delivered them from their peril by providing quail, manna, and water. When the people reached Sinai, God entered into Covenant relation with them. The essence of this relation is set forth in these words:

> "You have seen what I did to the Egyptians, and how I bore you on eagles' wings and brought you to myself. Now therefore, if you will obey my voice and keep my covenant, you shall be my own possession among all peoples; for all the earth is mine, and you shall be to me a kingdom of priests and a holy nation" (Exod. 19:4-6a).

The people responded: "All that the LORD has spoken we will do" (19:8; compare 24:3). The ratification of the Covenant is described in Exodus 24. The throwing of the blood on the people and the altar symbolizes the bond uniting the people in fellowship with God. The Covenant is sealed in blood. This close association of blood with covenant is carried over into the New Testament (I Cor. 11:25; Mark 14:22; Heb. 9:15-22). The sacrificial meal also symbolizes the establishment of the Covenant (Exod. 24:9-11); the Lord's Supper includes the symbolism of both blood and meal.

The Covenant rested upon God's mighty deliverance from Egypt, and the keeping of the Covenant on Israel's part meant obedience to God's will. A covenant is a binding of persons into a special reciprocal relationship. In the ancient Near Eastern world, covenants were frequently made. Sometimes the contracting parties were equals; at other times they were not equals. The Covenant of God with Israel was of the latter type. God was the initiator of the Covenant and made all the requirements. He first committed himself to the people and then called upon them to commit themselves to him.

This binding of God to his people is one of the chief facts which bind the two Testaments (covenants) together. Israel, as the Covenant people, was to be "a kingdom of priests and a holy nation." Not every individual Israelite could serve at the altar, but all Israel had a vocation to worship and serve God as a people set apart for a special task, which was to be made clearer as time went on.

The Covenant is best understood in the framework of election. Election is implicit throughout the history of Israel, though it is particularly strong in Deuteronomy and Isaiah 40-55. One of the clearest statements of this election is found in Deuteronomy 7:6-15, where it is evident that God elects a people and the Covenant itself out of his own mysterious love. He maintains the Covenant in his faithfulness and loving steadfastness. When election and Covenant are examined throughout the Old Testament, it is clear that Israel was elected to privilege, obedience, and service as the Covenant people. This Covenant relationship is forcefully described by several metaphors:

God		Israel
Redeemer .	Exod. 20:2; Deut. 7:8; Isa. 43:1	Redeemed
King	Exod. 19:5-6; Isa. 41:8-9; 43:15	Servant
Father . . .	Exod. 4:22; Hosea 11:1; Isa. 63:16	Son
Husband . .	Hosea 1-3; Jer. 2-3; Ezek. 16; Isa. 54	Wife
Vinedresser	Isa. 5; Ezek. 15:1-6; 19:10-14; Ps. 80:8-19	Vine
Potter	Jer. 18:1-11; Isa. 64:8	Clay
Shepherd .	Ezek. 34:11-31; Isa. 40:11; Pss. 80, 23 . .	Sheep

One expression of the Covenant was law. In Exodus this is indicated by the placing of the Ten Commandments (Exod. 20:1-17) and the Covenant Code (Exod. 20:22—23:33) in the midst of the Covenant ceremony itself. More basic than the Commandments themselves is the prologue to them: "I am the LORD your God, who brought you out of the land of Egypt, out of the house of bondage." Law operates within grace and is founded upon it. God redeemed his Chosen People from Egyptian bondage before the Law was given. This was an act of pure grace. Then he gave them the Law to tell them how to live as his special possession. Their relationship to him and to others was to be motivated by gratitude for what he had done for them. From the biblical point of view ethics should spring from gratitude to and trust in the God of grace. The Christian recognizes that he is created in Christ Jesus, not by good works but for good works (Eph. 2:10).

Because of their lack of faith the Covenant people wandered in the wilderness forty years until a new generation should arise, their life characterized by murmuring and rebellion. All the while God's presence in the midst of his people was represented by the

Tabernacle, a movable sanctuary, and the Ark of the Covenant. At the Tabernacle prayers were made and the people assembled. John 1:14 may be translated, "And the Word became flesh and *tabernacled* among us." As God's presence among his ancient people was associated with the Tabernacle, so he *tabernacled* among his people at a later time in the uniqueness of the Incarnation. Furthermore, some of the symbolism employed in Hebrews is drawn from the Tabernacle (see Hebrews 9 and 10).

It was God who guided his people in the wilderness (Num. 9:15-23). He had promised a land to Abraham's descendants, and through Joshua, Moses' successor, he fulfilled the promise. Deuteronomy, Joshua, Judges, I and II Samuel, and I and II Kings share the same interpretation of history. The essence of this view is: obedience to God results in blessing; disobedience results in cursing.

The conquest of Canaan involves historical, theological, and ethical issues which are not treated here. It is sufficient to state that the gift of the land was one of the mighty acts of God rehearsed in the confessions of Israel's faith. Earlier we noted the rehearsal made by Joshua when the Covenant was renewed at Shechem (Joshua 24). On all occasions of Covenant renewal the rehearsal of God's mighty deeds in the past spoke to the people of his mighty working in the present and future. Furthermore, the people committed themselves anew to God as the God of the Covenant. God had elected (chosen) his people; Joshua calls upon the people to choose God (24:14-15). When we as Christians rehearse the mighty acts of God through sermon, Scripture, song, or sacrament, we similarly commit ourselves anew to the God of the Covenant.

The period of the judges was a time marked by moral and religious degeneration (Judges 2:11) and anarchy. "Every man did what was right in his own eyes" (Judges 17:6b; 21:25b). The repeated theme of the Book of Judges is this: Israel did evil in the sight of the Lord; God gave his people into the hand of the enemy; the people cried for help to the Lord; and he raised up a judge (deliverer) to deliver them.

During the period of the judges there was already some concern in Israel to have a king like other nations (Judges 8:22-23; ch. 9). The request for a king came in the time of Samuel, who was a judge, prophet, and priest. Saul, Israel's first king, was a good soldier and, to some extent, made possible the greatness of

David. However, after he disobeyed God, his sense of rejection by Samuel and by God led him to melancholia and despair.

David was anointed by Samuel as Saul's successor. In spite of his many excellent qualities and notable achievements, he committed adultery and murder. When Nathan, the prophet, pronounced God's judgment upon him, David repented and was forgiven, but the consequences of his sin are a tragic story (see II Sam. 12-19). Yet in the long run God's covenant with David (II Sam. 7:8-16; 23:2-7) and the founding of the Holy City played a large part in the story of salvation.

God Judges His People

The fact that God judges is not new at this point in the biblical narrative, but it is most powerfully demonstrated in the period from Solomon to the Babylonian Captivity. Judgment is the work of the judge in establishing justice. The ultimate purpose of judgment in the Old Testament is salvation, as the following words from Isaiah 33:22 indicate:

> For the LORD is our judge, the LORD is our ruler,
> the LORD is our king; he will save us.

The judges in Israel's early history were primarily deliverers (saviors). To judge the poor means to deliver him from oppression, but to judge the oppressor means to punish him (Ps. 72:1-4). Judgment, then, has two prongs: one to save and the other to condemn. In Israel's history both of these aspects of judgment are seen, the negative aspect being more obvious in the period prior to the Babylonian Exile.

The judges, and Samuel, Saul, and David, were "charismatic" leaders; that is, they were specially endowed by God's Spirit for their tasks. But beginning with Solomon, kingship became a matter of inheritance. In spite of his reputation for wisdom, Solomon showed lack of wisdom in the oppressive measures he forced upon his people. Furthermore, the judgment of God was pronounced upon him especially for his support of the religions of his foreign wives (I Kings 11:1-40).

In the time of Rehoboam, Solomon's son and successor, the kingdom was divided into Northern Israel and Southern Judah because Rehoboam continued and increased the oppression which Solomon had begun. Jeroboam, the son of Nebat, led a revolt of the ten northern tribes and ruled as the first king of Northern Israel. He established a shrine at Dan and another at Bethel as rivals to the Solomonic Temple in Jerusalem and set up a golden calf (perhaps a pedestal for the invisible Yahweh) at each shrine. Though this was not necessarily an attempt to introduce polytheism, it actually encouraged the people to combine their religion with Baalism, which also made use of calf images in worship. Jeroboam therefore came to be known as the king who "made Israel to sin."

Though Moses, Samuel, Nathan, and others had been prophets, we take up the account of the prophets in a special way with Elijah. A prophet is a man called by God to speak or enact God's message to his people. The kings had ceased to be charismatic leaders; charismatic leadership was carried on through the prophets. Elijah was called by God to meet the challenge of Phoenician Baalism which was sponsored by Jezebel, wife of Ahab, king of Northern Israel (869-850 B.C.). This was a conflict between the historical religion of Israel and the fertility cult of the Phoenicians. Said the prophet on Mount Carmel: "How long will you go limping with two different opinions? If the LORD is God, follow him; but if Baal, then follow him" (I Kings 18:21). When Elijah fled from Jezebel, he found personal renewal at Sinai-Horeb where long ago God had made the Covenant with his people through Moses. When Ahab murdered Naboth and took his vineyard (I Kings 21), Elijah made it plain that not even the king could with impunity violate the Covenant in relation to his subjects, a lesson David had learned earlier.

The great prophets of the eighth century B.C. performed their ministries against the background of the Assyrian menace. Amos and Hosea prophesied primarily to Northern Israel, and Isaiah and Micah primarily to Southern Judah. The messages of these prophets may be summarized thus:

> Amos—The Righteousness of God
> Hosea—The Love of God
> Isaiah—The Holiness of God
> Micah—The Requirement of God

Amos is known as the prophet of the righteousness of God. However, there were those before Amos who had a concern for God's righteousness (see Gen. 18:25). Too, his contemporaries and successors in the prophetic ministry made the same emphasis. Righteousness is basically that which conforms to God's character as he has revealed himself. Men and nations are to deal with one another according to God's standards:

> But let justice roll down like waters,
>   and righteousness like an ever-flowing stream
>
> (Amos 5:24).

All the eighth-century prophets accuse their people of injustice and oppression, which are expressions of rebellion against the righteous God. For such sin the judgment of God as punishment rests upon his Chosen People (Amos 3:2). Pious ritual is no substitute for ethical behavior. The Messiah of the line of David (Isa. 9:2-7; 11:1-16) will reign in "justice and . . . righteousness" (Isa. 9:7):

> He shall not judge by what his eyes see,
>   or decide by what his ears hear;
> but with righteousness he shall judge the poor,
>   and decide with equity for the meek of the earth
>
> (Isa. 11:3-4).

According to Jeremiah 23:5-6 and 33:14-16 God will raise up for David a righteous Branch who will execute justice and righteousness in the land; his name will be "The LORD is our righteousness." As the righteous God, God revealed, through the eighth-century prophets, his special interest in redeeming the poor and the oppressed. However, it is in the great Prophet of the Exile that the tendency to identify God's righteousness with his grace becomes most pronounced. Here righteousness sometimes means God's salvation or redemption of his people (for example, Isa. 45:8, 23; 46:13; 51:5-6). Justification takes place through the Servant of the Lord, who makes "many to be accounted righteous" (Isa. 53:11). It is the righteousness of God in this dimension that Paul proclaims in Galatians and Romans.

As Amos stresses the righteousness of God, Hosea stresses his love; though God's love is by no means confined to the Book of Hosea. Many words are used in the Old Testament to express God's love, words which may be translated by such expressions as "election-love," "steadfast love," "compassion," and "grace." It was out of his mysterious love that God chose Israel (Deut. 7:6-11), and it was in his love that Israel could hope. In the Book of Hosea, God's steadfast love or loving faithfulness is emphasized. It is through Hosea's domestic tragedy—the infidelity of his wife

—that God reveals his own love for unfaithful Israel, who has played the harlot after the Baals. God will judge her for her sin, but on account of his steadfast love for her he will one day win her back to himself. Implicit in this doctrine of hope is the doctrine of the Remnant. This figure of husband and wife to depict God's love for his people is also found in other prophets (Jer. 2:2, 32; 3:1; 31:32; Ezek. 16, 23; Isa. 54:5; 62:4). The figure of father and son is used for the same purpose (Hosea 11:1; Isa. 63:16). The response of God's people as either wife or son is to be one of steadfast love, faithfulness, reverence, and obedience:

> For I desire steadfast love and not sacrifice,
>   the knowledge of God, rather than burnt offerings
>   (Hosea 6:6).

Steadfast love is devotion to God and to others. It is synonymous with the knowledge of God. This is not knowledge about God but a personal relationship with him. God has already committed himself to his people in steadfast love. When they respond to God in steadfast love, the relationship is one of joy. Sin is a lack of this knowledge of God or unfaithfulness to the Covenant (Hosea 4:1-3; Isa. 1:2-4), and such sinfulness expresses itself in specific sins: "[false] swearing, lying, killing, stealing, and committing adultery." Through "the cross of Hosea" God revealed his love for Israel; through the cross of Christ he revealed his love for all men.

The holiness of God is dwelt upon in the prophets. The word, coming from a root meaning "to be separate," means essentially "godness." Only God is holy in the fundamental sense. He is separate from all his creation and is alone in the category of deity. For God to swear by his holiness (Amos 4:2) is for him to swear by himself. Though he is other than man he is not aloof from his people (Hosea 11:9). Persons and things are holy as God sets them in a special relation to himself. Therefore, we speak of the Holy People, the Holy Place, the Holy Land, the Holy City, and the Holy Bible.

Isaiah was the prophet par excellence of holiness. In the year King Uzziah of Judah died, Isaiah had a vision of the heavenly King in his exaltation and glory (Isa. 6). Long before Isaiah's day Moses had stood on holy ground when God confronted him at the burning bush (Exod. 3:5). Isaiah was confronted by the holy God and forever after knew him as "the Holy One of Israel" (for example, Isa. 1:4; 5:19, 24; 10:17, 20; 12:6; 17:7; 29:19,

23; 30:11-12, 15; 31:1). In the presence of the holy God, he confessed his own sinfulness and the sinfulness of his people. This means that God's holiness includes his righteousness. In fact, Isaiah states this clearly in 5:16:

> But the LORD of hosts is exalted in justice,
>   and the Holy God shows himself holy in righteousness.

Holiness also includes God's forgiving love (compare Hosea 11:9). As the holy God he forgave Isaiah and gave him a message of forgiveness to share with others (Isa. 1:18-20; compare Pss. 32, 51). After his cleansing Isaiah was ready to hear the call of God: "Whom shall I send, and who will go for us?" He replied, "Here I am! Send me" (Isa. 6:8). The commission he received is hard to understand. It seems that his task was almost hopeless, for the people were to be unresponsive. The holy God would send severe judgment upon his people, and yet there would be a "holy seed" or "stump"; that is, a remnant through which God would work out his purpose of salvation. The holiness of God includes all aspects of his character and is associated with all his works.

Micah made some of the same emphases as Amos, Hosea, and Isaiah. He was unusually sensitive to the sufferings of the poor and announced God's special judgment upon the leaders of his people: princes, prophets, and priests. Eight centuries later One from Bethlehem (see Micah 5:2-9; Matt. 2:6; John 7:42) was also unusually sensitive to the sufferings of the poor (see Luke 1:46-55; 4:16-21; 6:20; 7:22; 14:13, 21; 18:22; 21:3; Mark 10:21; 12:43; Matt. 11:5; 19:21) and pronounced God's judgment upon the leaders of his people (Matt. 21:33-46; 23:1-39). In Micah 6:8 there is an excellent summary of eighth-century prophecy in the form of the divine requirement:

> He has showed you, O man, what is good;
>   and what does the LORD require of you
> but to do justice, and to love kindness,
>   and to walk humbly with your God?

The prophets of the seventh century B.C. performed their ministries against the background of the Babylonian (Chaldean) menace. Their prophecies were addressed primarily to Judah, since Northern Israel fell to the Assyrians in 721 B.C. The messages of these prophets may be summarized thus:

Zephaniah—The Day of the Lord
Nahum—The Destruction of Nineveh
Habakkuk—A Call to Faith
Jeremiah—The New Covenant

The people of the eighth century expected the Day of the Lord to be a time when their enemies would be overthrown and they themselves would be blessed; but instead it would be a time of calamity for Israel (Amos 5:18-20; compare Isa. 2:6—3:26). However, such a Day of judgment would not be confined to Israel (Isa. 13; Ezek. 30). Of all the prophetic books Zephaniah contains the strongest emphasis upon the Day of the Lord as a day of wrath upon Judah and Jerusalem and upon all men. But this final Day is not associated with punishment alone, for it will issue in the Kingdom of God (Hosea 2:16-23; Isa. 2:1-5; 24:21-23; Micah 4:1-4; Zeph. 3:9-20; Mal. 4; Joel 1-3; Zech. 14; Ps. 98:9). In the New Testament the Day of the Lord becomes the Day of Christ (II Cor. 1:14; Phil. 1:6, 10), which will be a Day of judgment and wrath (Matt. 10:15; Rom. 2:5, 16; Jude 6) as a prelude to the consummation of the Kingdom.

The Book of Nahum illustrates the judgment of God through the prediction of a particular historical event, namely the destruction of Nineveh, the capital of the Assyrian Empire. God takes the evil of "the bloody city" (3:1) seriously.

Habakkuk was a prophet whom God called to a deeper faith. Of course all the true prophets were men of faith; they could not have been prophets otherwise. Perhaps it was harder to exercise faith in Habakkuk's day than it had been in the preceding century. Although King Josiah had carried out a religious reform, supported by the discovery of the Book of the Law in the Temple (621 B.C.), after his death the people began to return to their pagan customs. The reformation had demolished foreign altars but had not transformed the hearts of the people. In this situation Habakkuk found himself with questions concerning the righteousness of God. In effect he said: "O Lord, why do you let such great wrongs in Judah go unpunished?" God answered, "I am rousing the Chaldeans as instruments of my judgment." But this answer only deepened Habakkuk's problem: "The Chaldeans are more wicked than my own people. How can you as the righteous God allow the wicked to swallow up the man more righteous than he?" "I will judge the Chaldeans, Habakkuk, 'but the righteous shall live by his faith.' " The word translated "faith" (Hab. 2:4) includes both faith and faithfulness. God called Habakkuk to trust, even though he could not fully understand God's providence, and to be faithful to him regardless of circumstance. In other words, this was a call to a wholehearted commitment. Paul took Habakkuk 2:4b as his text in setting forth his doctrine of justification by faith (Gal. 3:11; Rom. 1:17).

The most distinctive aspect of Jeremiah's message is his doctrine of the New Covenant. Without the words Hosea seems to have preached the message of the New Covenant (2:19-20), but it remained for Jeremiah to make explicit that which was implicit. In the earlier years of his ministry Jeremiah had some hope of his people's repentance, but the time came when he saw that captivity for them was the will of God as punishment for their sin. This calamity did come, for Judah was taken captive by Babylon and the Temple was destroyed in 587 B.C. Yet, doom was not Jeremiah's final word. In Judah's darkest hour he bought a field in his home town, Anathoth, indicating thereby that there would be a return from captivity and that "houses and fields and vineyards" would "again be bought in this land" (Jer. 32:1-44; 29: 1-14). His announcement of the New Covenant is one of the peaks of Old Testament prophecy (31:31-34). According to this announcement God's will will be written on the heart, and life's motivations will be internal. Men will know God in personal commitment to him and will experience the forgiveness of sin. Yet this knowledge of God will operate within the community of the Covenant, not in selfish isolation. The theme of the New Covenant was carried on by Ezekiel (16:60-63; 34:25) and the great Prophet of the Exile (Isa. 53:3-5; 61:8).

The Remnant

God chose Israel as the instrument of his saving purpose, but not all Israel responded in obedience to God. Therefore, God's purpose was carried on through a Remnant. As the story of salvation has moved from creation to the Remnant, the hourglass has narrowed considerably. Rather than removing God's people from judgment, election placed them under judgment in a special way (Amos 3:2).

God Preserves a Remnant

The concept of the Remnant is expressed in a variety of ways by the prophets. It cuts in two ways at the same time, the way of punishment and the way of salvation. Isaiah named one of his sons Shearjashub, "a remnant shall return." This can mean "only a remnant shall return" or "beyond a shadow of a doubt a remnant shall return" (Isa. 7:3). The Remnant is associated with punishment and destruction in such passages as Amos 3:12 and 5:3. It is associated with salvation in such passages as Isaiah 11:11, 16 and 46:3. Both positive and negative aspects are expanded in Isaiah 10:20-23. Here the Remnant will turn to God in repentance, and at the same time only a Remnant will return. After the fall of the Northern Kingdom to Assyria, Judah is sometimes considered the Remnant (II Kings 17:18; 21:14-15; Isa. 37:31-32).

At other times the Remnant is composed of Judah and those in Northern Israel who escaped the Assyrian Captivity (II Chron. 30:6). In Amos 5:15 the term is used to apply only to the Northern Israelite survivors of catastrophe. Jeremiah divides the survivors of the fall of Jerusalem into two Remnants, those who go into exile to Babylon, and those who remain in Judah together with those who go to Egypt (chapter 24). He sees the Babylonian Remnant as the Remnant that repents. Yet, in Jeremiah 23:3 we read: "Then [in the Messianic Age] I will gather the remnant of my flock out of all the countries where I have driven them . . ." Already in the eighth century Isaiah had prophesied that God would recover the Remnant of his people from various lands in the Messianic Age (11:11-16). Zephaniah seems to say that the humble will be the Remnant in the Day of the Lord (2:3; compare Micah 4:7). Ezekiel looks forward to the heart renewal of the exiled Remnant that returns to the Promised Land (11:13-20). The Prophet of the Exile promises the Remnant in exile that God will save them (Isa. 46:3-4). In Haggai (1:12-14), Zechariah (8:6, 11-12), and Ezra (9:8, 15) the Remnant is composed of the returned exiles.

This Remnant does not exclude the Jews already living in Judah (Neh. 1:3). According to Zephaniah 3:9 and Zechariah 14:16 the ultimate Remnant will include people from other nations. In the final judgment the Remnant will be those "who call upon the name of the LORD"; that is, "those whom the LORD calls" (Joel 2:32). The human complement to God's election is faith. Peter uses this verse in his sermon on the Day of Pentecost (Acts 2:21) and Paul uses it in Romans 10:13. Though no word for "Remnant" is used, the idea is present in Daniel 12:1-4, where some of those raised from the dead belong to the redeemed Remnant. In the light of this brief survey, it is evident that the period from the Babylonian Captivity to the time of Jesus is in a real sense the period of the Remnant.

The Babylonian Exile brought suffering to the Jews (Ps. 137), yet it was a time when real gains were made. One important gain was made when the Remnant, which was the true Israel, learned to live without the Temple and the Jewish state.

God Comforts the Exiles

In the period of exile and restoration God spoke to his people through three prophets, each with a distinctive message:

>   Obadiah—Retribution upon Edom
>   Ezekiel—The Glory of the Lord
>   Isaiah 40-66—The Servant of the Lord

Though the exact date of Obadiah is uncertain, his prophecy seems to come from the sixth century. He announced the judgment of God upon the Edomites, the ancient enemy of Israel and Judah. God's comfort for the exiles was given primarily through Ezekiel and the Prophet of the Exile.

Ezekiel was a priest who was carried into exile in the deportation of 597 B.C. In 592 B.C. he was called to the prophetic ministry. From the time of his call he lived in the consciousness of the Glory of the Lord (Ezek. 1:28—2:10). God's glory is the combination of his honor, dignity, splendor, and excellence which call forth reverence, humility, praise, and obedience—the manifestation of God's holiness. Ezekiel responded to God's glory by prostrating himself; in such a presence he was but mortal man. According to the other great prophet in this period, God's glory will be revealed in the future in such a way that "all flesh shall see it together" (Isa. 40:5). The Christian cannot help thinking of the words of Paul: "For it is the God who said, 'Let light shine out of darkness,' who has shone in our hearts to give the light of the knowledge of the glory of God in the face of Christ" (II Cor. 4:6).

For the most part Ezekiel's ministry was carried on among his fellow exiles. Before the fall of Jerusalem his message was one of judgment upon Jerusalem, but after the fall it was one of hope. He was called to be a watchman to warn the wicked and the righteous. Like Isaiah, he stressed the holiness and transcendence of God; and, like Jeremiah, he stressed individual responsibility. The exiles claimed that their captivity was the result of their fathers' sin and consequently unmerited. But Ezekiel pointed out the personal responsibility of the exiles themselves (Ezek. 18; 33:1-20). He called his people to repentance and forgiveness. His doctrine of salvation includes a new heart (11:19; 36:26), a new life (37), a new Covenant (34:25; 36:27), a new David (34:20-24; 37:24-28), a new Temple (40-48), and a new Jerusalem (40-48).

Old Testament prophecy reaches its peak in Isaiah 40-66. Almost all the theology of the rest of the Old Testament is integrated here at the highest level. All is placed in an eschatological setting, that is, at the end of the Old Age and the beginning of the New. There will be a new Exodus (52:11-12), a new Covenant (53:3-5), a new Jerusalem (54:11-15), and a new creation (51:1-16; 65:17; 66:22). God will redeem his people in a second Exodus, and he will judge his people's enemies. Israel's Redeemer is also her Creator and the Creator of the heavens and the earth. He will redeem his people not only from literal exile but also from bondage to sin. His mighty works as Redeemer and Creator reveal his universal kingship. Cyrus the Persian has been raised up by him to set his people free. He is the only God, and "there is no other" (Isa. 45:5, 14). He is the Holy One of Israel, who has chosen Israel to be his servant. Israel has been elected to a missionary responsibility as well as to privilege (43:10; 51:4). She is to declare to the nations that the Lord is "a righteous God and a Savior" and that there is none besides him (45:21; compare 45:22-23). God's promise to Abraham (51:2) and his covenant with David (55:3) will be fulfilled.

The Servant of the Lord plays a large part in the message of this prophet. Sometimes the Servant is clearly designated as Israel, but at other times he is not named. He is Israel and at the same time he is the individual Israelite in the highest form. As Israel, the unnamed Servant has a mission to the nations (42:6-7; 49:6); yet, he also has a redemptive mission to Israel (49:5). The greatest of the Servant Songs and one of the greatest passages in all Scripture is Isaiah 52:13—53:12. Here it is learned that the Servant will ultimately be raised and exalted, but before his exaltation he must go through deep humiliation.

In this great poem there is an emphasis upon the gospel for the whole man as a suffering and dying sinner. The Servant vicariously bears suffering as well as sin. Yet sin is the core of the problem of evil, and various approaches to its forgiveness are brought together. First, there is the priestly approach of substitutionary sacrifice, resting in part upon the meaning of some of the Temple ritual. Life comes only through death. This is a principle which also applies even in a less profound sense than is intended here. Biologically, human beings live out of the death of animals and plants. Some of us are biologically alive because others have died for us in war or in scientific experiment. But at the profound level of which the prophet is speaking, we have "eternal" life only through the death of the Servant of the Lord.

Second, there is the prophetic approach of confession and repentance: "all we like sheep have gone astray" (compare 55:6-7). It is implied that the "many" who are justified (53:11) are those who confess their sins. Finally, there is the approach of prayerful intercession. The Servant intercedes for those who are responsible for his death (compare Gen. 18:22-32; Exod. 32:9-14; Amos 7:1-6; II Chron. 30:18-19). Christians have rightly seen in Jesus the fulfillment of the prophecies concerning the Servant.

God Brings His People Home

In 538 B.C., Cyrus the Persian made a proclamation permitting the Jewish exiles who so desired to return to their homeland. A group did return under Sheshbazzar, a Davidic prince, who laid the foundation of the Temple in Jerusalem. But the work on the Temple was stopped. Haggai and Zechariah encouraged the people to complete the rebuilding of the house of the Lord. The leadership of the community was centered in Zerubbabel, the successor to Sheshbazzar, and Joshua, the son of the high priest. Under Zerubbabel's leadership the Temple was rebuilt.

In thinking of the Temple, it is appropriate to recall that the Psalter has often been called "the hymnbook of the second Temple." This does not mean that all or most of the Psalms were composed in the period after the Babylonian Exile, but that many of them were used in the worship of the second Temple. The composition of the Psalms extends from pre-Davidic times to the fourth century B.C. In the Psalms the whole theology of Israel is set to music. Here the people of God respond in the various attitudes and acts of worship to the revelation of God through history, prophecy, law, and wisdom.

Shortly after the time of Zerubbabel the walls of Jerusalem

were rebuilt under the leadership of Nehemiah in spite of strong opposition from Samaritans and others. Ezra led another group of exiles back to Jerusalem and conducted a drastic reform among his people. In order to prevent a reversion to paganism, he forced all Jews who had married non-Jewish wives to send their wives away. But Ezra's reform also had its positive aspects. From Babylon he had brought with him the Book of the Law, which was probably the Pentateuch (Genesis, Exodus, Leviticus, Numbers, Deuteronomy). He read the Law to the people and they renewed the Covenant with God. Ezra's Covenant prayer (Neh. 9) is a marvelous review of God's mighty acts in the story of salvation from creation to Ezra's own time. At this point in history the Pentateuch became canonical, and the people of God became the people of the Law.

No doubt Ezra did the best he knew in requiring the Jews to send their foreign wives back home. But there were those who seem to have had a different point of view. Had not the great Prophet of the Exile (Isa. 40-66) announced that Israel was to be a missionary servant to the nations? Both the Book of Ruth and the Book of Jonah are relevant to this issue. The Book of Ruth has its setting in the time of the judges. Ruth, a Moabitess, marries Boaz, an Israelite, and becomes the great-grandmother of King David himself. In the Book of Jonah the attitude of the Jews toward non-Jews is typified by Jonah. God shows Jonah that there are some good things about the pagan sailors whom he encounters on board ship and that he, God, is concerned about the repentance of the worst enemies of his people.

Although some of the exiles had returned to Jerusalem, and the Temple had been rebuilt, and the Covenant renewed, the postexilic community was not the complete fulfillment anticipated by the prophets of former years. The Zion of God's glory was yet to be.

God Speaks to His People Through Wisdom and Apocalypse

The Wisdom Literature of the Old Testament (chiefly Proverbs, Ecclesiastes, Job, and a few Psalms) is not as closely related to the events of history as the Law and the Prophets. The materials placed in this category had a long history before they were collected and put in their final form in the postexilic period. Wisdom Literature has characterized all societies, both ancient and modern. It tends to concentrate upon the individual as he faces the facts of everyday experience. Within it are practical advice to the young and serious reflection on life's hard problems. Proverbs is composed largely of practical advice, whereas Ecclesiastes and Job are more reflective. Wisdom Literature is the closest thing in the Old Testament to philosophy. Its points of reference are human experience and nature. Yet wisdom is the gift of God. Perhaps its relationship to the Law and the Prophets is most clearly seen in such Psalms as 1, 19, 119, 128, and 133.

The Book of Job is one of the greatest pieces of literature in the libraries of mankind. It is the voice of man crying out in the anguish of suffering: "Why?" It is also the voice of God answering the sufferer. The connection between suffering and sin has already been noted. Suffering is a significant theme in various parts of the Old Testament. Although it is placed in the category of evil, it may serve the purposes of justice (Deut. and the Prophets), education (Prov. 3:11; Job 32-37), testing (Hab. and Isa. 48:10), warning to repent (Amos 4:6-12), revelation (Hosea), redemption (Isa. 52:13—53:12), and hope (Isa. 24-27 and Daniel).

The question of the Prologue to the Book of Job is, "Does Job fear God for nought?" (1:9). That is, Will a man be devoted to God if he does not receive material and physical blessings from God? In essence the personal question of Job himself is, "Why do you, the righteous and all-powerful God, cause me, a righteous man, to suffer the loss of all things, including my health?" Job's friends tell him that his suffering is in proportion to his sinning, but Job insists upon his integrity. The question of the book is answered thus: Yes, Job does fear God for nought *but God himself;* even when he has been stripped of everything, he maintains his faith in God. Job's personal question is not answered on the intellectual level; rather, Job is answered. It is given to man to live by faith. The mystery of evil remains a mystery, but in the divine-human encounter Job is found of God and finds himself:

> I had heard of thee by the hearing of the ear,
>   but now my eye sees thee;
> therefore I despise myself,
>   and repent in dust and ashes (42:5-6).

Job had been living on a secondhand religion. He was not suffering from God's judgment upon his sin; nevertheless, in his encounter with God he did recognize himself to be a sinner and turned from his pride and arrogance to the arms of God. When

God comes to us and we turn to him, we may still have unanswered questions but we ourselves have been answered at the deepest level of communication.

Although the formal setting of the Book of Daniel is laid in the sixth century B.C., its message is directed to the Jews suffering under the severe persecution of Antiochus Epiphanes in the second century. The book belongs to the literary classification known as apocalypse or revelation, which is characterized by the use of symbols and visions and by both wisdom and prophetic emphases. In Daniel the author gives a profound interpretation of history. He sees the Kingdom of God as past, present, and future. God is always the sovereign Lord of men and nations, but his people ("the saints of the Most High") will experience a climactic expression of his sovereignty in their reception of the Kingdom. The heavenly man, who is described as "one like a son of man" in chapter 7, may be a personalized representation of "the saints of the Most High." Yet, in a short time the expression "son of man" comes to be interpreted individually in the Intertestament literature (I Enoch 46:2, 4; etc.). In the struggle against persecution God's people are to live in defiant faith, no matter what happens to them, for their security lies in the hands of the eternal God who will even raise the dead.

We have followed the account of God's mighty acts in hourglass fashion from creation to the Fall, to the election of the Chosen People, to the Remnant, and we know God has been speaking to us. We kneel before him in reverence, gratitude, and steadfast love. We realize that with all its wisdom and beauty, the Old Testament by itself is a promise to be fulfilled. We feel we are standing on the very border of a Promised Land. The new David, the new Age, the new Covenant, and the new Israel are about to enter the drama of human history.

The One—Jesus Christ

"God Sent Forth His Son"

"But when the time had fully come, God sent forth his Son, born of woman, born under the law, to redeem those who were under the law, so that we might receive adoption as sons" (Gal. 4:4-5). God, in working out his purpose, moved from creation to the One who fulfilled the hope of his people.

At the time of Jesus' birth this hope was variously expressed among the Jewish people. The party known as the Sadducees had no Messianic hope. The Pharisees, their antagonists, believed that if the Jews observed the Law strictly, God would bring in the Kingdom under a Davidic Messiah. The Zealots longed for a military Messiah who would throw off the Roman yoke. The Apocalyptists, who lived in the tradition of such books as Daniel and I Enoch, expected the heavenly Son of Man to receive the eternal Kingdom. The Essenes or Essene-like people of the Dead Sea Scrolls seem to have expected three Messianic figures: a prophet, a priestly Messiah, and a Davidic Messiah.

We saw at the beginning of this study that the Apostles preached Jesus as the Christ (Messiah), the Son of David. All the writers of the New Testament were certain of the identification. Jesus was hesitant about the use of the title (Mark 8:30), but he clearly acknowledged it before the Jewish Council (Mark 14:62). He was not an exact duplicate of David; he would set up no political kingdom and make no war on Rome. Rather he dramatized the fact that he was the Messiah of peace by his triumphal entry into Jerusalem on a donkey ' (Matt. 21:1-11; compare Zech. 9:9).

Jesus' favorite title for himself was the Son of Man. Sometimes the expression clearly refers to Jesus as a person; at other times it seems to refer to the people belonging to him. In other words, there is a kind of fluidity in the expression which ties Jesus and his followers together. The background of this title has already been found in Daniel and I Enoch. Some think the Son of Man had already been identified with the Messiah before the time of Jesus, but it is clear that Jesus united the two concepts. When the high priest asked him, "Are you the Christ, the Son of the Blessed?" he said, "I am; and you will see the Son of man sitting at the right hand of Power, and coming with the clouds of heaven" (Mark 14:61-62).

We have seen that the people of the Dead Sea Scrolls community probably expected a "messianic" prophet, a priestly Messiah, and a Davidic Messiah. The prophet was not a third Messiah but an eschatological figure. According to John 1:21; 6:14; and 7:40 there was generally among the Jews expectation of a prophet. In the days of his flesh Jesus was recognized as a prophet by the Apostles, who saw in him a prophet like Moses in fulfillment of Deuteronomy 18:15-22 (Matt. 21:11; Acts 3:22; 7:37). But Jesus is superior to Moses and he is the mediator of a covenant that is superior to the Mosaic Covenant (Heb. 3:1-6; 12:18-24). As the new Moses, Jesus came to call men to surrender to the will of God from within.

Jesus is clearly presented as the priestly Messiah in the Letter to the Hebrews. Here Psalm 110 is used as the Old Testament background for interpreting Jesus as the priestly and royal Messiah, of whom Melchizedek is the type (compare Gen. 14:17-20). As a priest after the order of Melchizedek Jesus exercises a priesthood that has no end.

The Dead Sea Scrolls community expected a Davidic Messiah who would lead his people against their enemies in the final conflict of history. Although Jesus was Prophet, Priest, and King, he so transformed and enriched each concept with which he was associated that it could never be altogether the same again.

Jesus claimed a unique Sonship in relation to the Father (Matt. 11:27; compare Mark 8:38), and the Apostles in their preaching acknowledged him as Son of God and Lord. Both Paul and John proclaimed the pre-existence of Christ (Phil. 2:5-11; John 1: 1-5). In John 1 he is the eternal Word of God, personal and divine, the agent of creation, the source of life and light. As the Son of God he is "the image of the invisible God, the first-born of all creation" (Col. 1:15). That is, he is the visible revelation of the invisible God and the one who reigned before creation. In fact, he is deity itself (Titus 2:13; John 1:1; II Peter 1:1).

Jesus understood himself to be the Servant of the Lord, and his disciples came to his understanding eventually. According to the Gospel of Mark (1:11) he understood himself to be the Messiah and Servant of the Lord from the time of his baptism. The voice from heaven said: "Thou art my beloved Son; with thee I am well pleased." The first part of this quotation comes from Psalm 2:7, a Psalm regarded as Messianic; the second part comes from Isaiah 42:1, a passage dealing with the Servant of the Lord. Jesus fulfilled the mission of the Messiah, who was also the Servant of the Lord. In Mark 10:45 he interprets his mission as the Son of Man in terms of the mission of the Servant: "For the Son of man also came not to be served but to serve, and to give his life as a ransom for many." In Isaiah 52:13—53:12 the Servant, in his humiliation and exaltation, is anticipated; in Philippians 2:5-11 he is announced; and in Mark 8:34-36 he calls his disciples to the pattern of the servant life.

Jesus Served, Died, and Was Raised

Jesus' birth of a virgin and his early years are covered in the Gospels of Matthew (1-2) and Luke (1-2). As the forerunner (Matt. 11:10; compare Mal. 3:1) of the Mighty One, John the Baptist preached, "Repent, for the kingdom of heaven is at hand" (Matt. 3:2). He preached "a baptism of repentance for the forgiveness of sins" (Mark 1:4). In permitting himself to be baptized by John, Jesus seems to have identified himself with the people he had come to save. His temptation experience (Matt. 4:1-11; Luke 4:1-13) served as a further preparation for his ministry.

Jesus performed a ministry of the compassionate deed as he healed the sick, cleansed the leper, and raised the dead; a ministry of the spoken word as he preached and taught the Kingdom of God; and a ministry of the given life as he made his pilgrimage from Bethlehem to Calvary. All that he did must be seen against the background of the Kingdom. The Kingdom may be called the kingly rule of God, the kingship of God, and the realm of God's reign. It was present in the person, life, mighty deeds (Luke 11:20), death, and resurrection of Jesus the Messiah.

Jesus in his preaching and teaching was concerned with the Kingdom. Mark summarizes his preaching thus: "The time is fulfilled, and the kingdom of God is at hand; repent, and believe in the gospel" (1:15). This does not mean that the Kingdom has been fully consummated but that it has begun to arrive. In view of this fact men are exhorted to turn from their sin to God, that is, to reorient their lives and to respond in faith to the good news which Jesus brings. The Kingdom is both present (Luke 11:20) and future (Mark 14:25). It is to be sought (Matt. 6:33); yet it is a gift of the Father (Luke 12:32).

The ethical teachings of Jesus are expressions of the life of the Kingdom (see Matt. 5-7; compare Luke 6:20-49; 12:22-31; 11:9-13). They are not a means by which one is justified but an expression of the life already committed to the King. These teachings are not to be brushed aside as impracticable in the modern world, nor are they to be treated legalistically. "You, therefore, must be perfect, as your heavenly Father is perfect" (Matt. 5:48) is no idle statement. It throws us on the mercy of God. The Messiah could set nothing less than perfection as the standard of Kingdom living.

The message of the Kingdom will produce some positive results (the parable of the Sower, Matt. 13:3-9). The parable of the

Mustard Seed (Matt. 13:31-32) gives assurance of the extension of the Kingdom, and the parable of the Leaven (Matt. 13:33) an assurance of its permeation of society. The Kingdom is at the top of the disciple's priority list (Matt. 6:33; Luke 14:26; 9:62). The Messiah identifies himself with the person in need, and our treatment of the needy is our treatment of him (Matt. 25:31-46).

In some cases Jesus' teaching was in line with that of his predecessors, but he had a way of distinguishing that which is central from the marginal. Furthermore, he is the only teacher who ever lived perfectly what he taught. He gave love a new dimension. The disciple is to love his enemy (Matt. 5:44-47; Luke 6:27-28, 32-36). Many people in Jesus' day agreed that the two great commandments are to love God with all one's being and one's neighbor as oneself (Matt. 22:34-40 and parallels), but few, if any, would have defined "neighbor" as Jesus did in the parable of the Good Samaritan (Luke 10:29-37).

Closely related to loving one's enemy is forgiving an offender. No limit is to be placed on the number of times a disciple forgives another (Luke 17:3-4). The person who will not forgive cannot himself expect forgiveness from God (Matt. 6:12). Forgiveness is rooted in the character of the forgiving Father (Luke 15:11-32).

Disciples are also to be characterized by humility and service. James and John asked Jesus to give them the seats of honor in his Kingdom, but Jesus told them, "Whoever would be great among you must be your servant, and whoever would be first among you must be slave of all" (Mark 10:43-44; compare Luke 14:8-10).

The Kingdom is not a matter of biological descent (Matt. 21:43) or social position. Tax collectors and harlots enter it before the chief priests and elders (Matt. 21:31). The new wine of the Kingdom cannot be contained in the old wineskins of traditionalism (Mark 2:22).

Jesus' ministry included the ministry of the given life. "My food is to do the will of him who sent me, and to accomplish his work" (John 4:34), he said. His life throughout was dedicated to the Father's will. Increasingly he was opposed by the Pharisees and Sadducees, and he anticipated the suffering and death which lay ahead. He loved the people who had rejected him: "O Jerusalem, Jerusalem . . . How often would I have gathered your children together as a hen gathers her brood under her wings, and you would not!" (Matt. 23:37; Luke 13:34).

The Last Supper of Jesus with his innermost circle of disciples

(Mark 14:12-31; Matt. 26:17-30; Luke 22:7-23; I Cor. 11:23-26) has been of first importance to the Church through the years. It is associated with the Passover season. As the Jewish Passover was the sacrament of Israel's redemption from Egyptian bondage, so the Supper was the sacrament of a more profound deliverance, for it was interpretive of Jesus' death, which would soon take place. The bread represented his body and the cup his blood. The Old Covenant had been sealed by blood (Exod. 24:8), and Jesus was to pour out his life for many. He thought of himself as fulfilling Jeremiah's prophecy of the New Covenant (Jer. 31:31-34): "This cup is the new covenant in my blood" (I Cor. 11:25). Somehow this meal was prophetic of the consummation of the Kingdom (Mark 14:25; I Cor. 11:26).

Throughout the New Testament Jesus' death is interpreted as making atonement for sin. But this does not mean that his death in this regard stands apart from his incarnation, life, and resurrection. The mighty acts of God in Christ are all parts of the one drama of redemption. Atonement is the means by which right relations with God are effected. These presuppositions underlie this doctrine: (1) God and man should be at one; (2) God is holy love; (3) man is a rebel against God; and (4) God judges the rebel.

Without using the word, we have already been thinking about atonement in the discussion of the Servant of the Lord, in the mention of "ransom" in Mark 10:45, and in the treatment of the Last Supper. Jesus died *in behalf* of others (Mark 14:24; I Cor. 15:3; Rom. 8:32; Heb. 2:9; John 10:15); *in the place* of others (Mark 10:45; II Cor. 5:21; I Peter 1:18; 2:24); and as the *representative* of others (II Cor. 5:14; Rom. 5:19). Furthermore, that his death was sacrificial is evident in the concept of the Servant, in the accounts of the Last Supper, and throughout the New Testament. Jesus is "our paschal lamb" (I Cor. 5:7), "an expiation [or mercy seat] by his blood" (Rom. 3:25), "a fragrant offering and sacrifice to God" (Eph. 5:2), high priest and offering (Hebrews), and "the Lamb of God, who takes away the sin of the world" (John 1:29). The Cross was the necessary issue of Jesus' way of life, for it is only as "a grain of wheat falls into the earth and dies" that "it bears much fruit" (John 12:24). The revelation of God's love in the "lifted up" Jesus has tremendous power to draw men to him (John 12:32). The poured-out life of Christ, offered through eternal Spirit, purifies the conscience "from dead works to serve the living God" (Heb. 9:14). By his suffering Jesus gave us an example of how to face crises (I Peter 2:21). The disciple's cross means death to self-centeredness and surrender to Christ (Matt. 16:24). Through the death of Jesus, God was mightily at work in our behalf.

Although Jesus was and is the Son of God, the Gospels make it equally clear that he was truly man (see especially John 1:14; compare I John 4:2; II John 7). He was the Son of Mary, the Son of David, the Son of Abraham, and the Son of Adam. He "increased in wisdom and in stature, and in favor with God and man" (Luke 2:52). His teachings are filled with a knowledge of everyday affairs in first-century Palestine. He hungered, grew weary, and slept. He claimed ignorance of the time of the consummation of the Kingdom (Mark 13:32). He was tempted in every respect as we are (Heb. 4:15). He lived as a man of prayer and faith. His suffering and death were real. There was no hypocrisy in his humanity. Yet, which of us can convict him of sin? His temptation, unlike ours, did not issue in sinning. Even as we behold the manhood of the Master, we are constrained to cry, "This man is the Son of God!" As the God-man he bound God and men of faith together in the Covenant of God's eternal love.

The early preaching of the Apostles as recorded in Acts and I Corinthians 15:3-8 centered in the death and resurrection of Jesus. This preaching was done by personal witnesses. The very existence of the Christian Church is testimony to Christ's resurrection. The discouraged and fearful Apostles (for example, Peter, who had denied him) were transformed into men of fearless courage. The Resurrection prepared the way for the events of Pentecost. The accounts of the Resurrection in the four Gospels bear the marks of dependability. Each writer tells the story in his own way, yet it is essentially the same story, with no evidence of mechanical fabrication.

Jesus' death and resurrection are the interpreting center of the entire New Testament. Incarnation, ministry, death, and resurrection are all of one piece. Christians began to worship on the first day of the week, which they called the Lord's Day, because he was raised on that day. Every week the Christian celebrates a little Easter. Transformed lives, homes, and institutions through the centuries add their witness to the power of his resurrection. Only the resurrection of Jesus can account for the shout of victory over suffering, sin, and death that has resounded from the first Christian Easter to the present day. This is the crowning act of God that gives ultimate meaning to the historical process and to the life of each person in it.

The Apostles

The story of salvation now broadens from the One to the Apostles and other early disciples. They were the Remnant who received him. Jesus brought into being the people of the New Covenant through his person, ministry, death, and resurrection. As the Messiah of the Kingdom he called into being a people over whom he ruled. As Teacher, Preacher, and Prophet he had a people who received his word. As Shepherd he had a "little flock," to whom the Father gives the Kingdom (Matt. 26:31; Luke 12:32). As the Servant of the Lord he gathered those about him who were to live in-behalf-of lives. With the authority of love he chose twelve men from among his disciples and designated them Apostles. He trained them carefully, sent them forth, bound himself to them in the New Covenant, and promised to be with them.

Jesus seems to have chosen twelve because there were twelve tribes in Old Israel, thereby indicating that they were the nucleus of the New Israel. In the Early Church the Twelve were of special significance as leaders. They were *the* Apostles. The word "apostle" means "one sent forth"; that is, a missionary. The Twelve were missionaries, but they also exercised a general leadership over the other disciples. The expression was very quickly applied to others outside the Twelve, including Paul. Acts 1:8 describes how the Christian mission got under way: "But you shall receive power when the Holy Spirit has come upon you; and you shall be my witnesses in Jerusalem and in all Judea and Samaria and to the end of the earth."

On the Day of Pentecost the Holy Spirit came in special power upon the 120 who waited expectantly with one accord and in one place. Though some of God's choicest blessings will come to us only as we go into the closet and pray to our Heavenly Father in secret, other blessings will come only when we are together in one accord and in one place. The sanctuary and the closet are complementary. The disciples were all filled with the Holy Spirit and were able to witness to Christ as never before. Peter preached his famous sermon, and three thousand were baptized.

The early disciples recognized themselves as the people of God to whom the prophetic promises were being fulfilled (Acts 3:25). "They devoted themselves to the apostles' teaching and fellowship, to the breaking of bread and the prayers" (Acts 2:42). They were concerned for one another. They worshiped in the Temple as well as in their homes, for the Christian movement had not yet broken with Judaism. Nevertheless, it was not long before Peter, John, Stephen, and others ran into trouble with the authorities, and Stephen became the first Christian martyr. The word "martyr" is the transliteration of the Greek word for "witness." Soon many Christians were to bear witness to Christ through martyrdom, especially under Roman persecution. The way of the Cross is not easy in any generation, but it is glorious.

The Church

The hourglass broadens from the small Remnant of disciples to the full-fledged Christian fellowship. The origin of the Church can be accounted for only in relation to God's purpose as expressed through Israel, the Remnant, Jesus Christ, Jesus' Apostles and disciples, and the work of the Holy Spirit. The usual New Testament word for "church" has associations in the Greek Old Testament with the people of God. In the New Testament it refers to the people of the New Covenant, namely those to whom the promises of God are fulfilled. A local congregation is the expression of the whole people of God, not an isolated unit.

In addition to the word "church" there are several expressions which describe the people of the New Covenant in relation to the people of the Old: "the Israel of God" (Gal. 6:16; compare Rom. 9:6); "Abraham's offspring" (Gal. 3:29); "the twelve tribes" (James 1:1); "the exiles" (I Peter 1:1); "the household of God" (I Tim. 3:15); "a spiritual house" (I Peter 2:5); "a holy priesthood" (I Peter 2:5); "a chosen race, a royal priesthood, a holy nation, God's own people" (I Peter 2:9). Furthermore, the Church may be thought of as believers who have fellowship with Christ and with one another in Christ. In fact, the Church may be called a fellowship which expresses itself in sharing Christ.

Jesus Mediates the New Covenant

The relationship between God and his people under the New Covenant is expressed under the same figures used to describe this relationship under the Old Covenant (see previous discussion of the Covenant). *God is the Redeemer and his people are the redeemed*. This is the meaning of the Benedictus in Luke 1:68-69:

> "Blessed be the Lord God of Israel,
> for he has visited and redeemed his people,
> and has raised up a horn of salvation for us."

Through Jesus, the incarnate Redeemer, God's redemptive purpose is worked out in history. That to which the Old Testament pointed has become actual in the person and work of Jesus. Men are in bondage to sin and legalism, but they are set free through him and adopted into the family of God (Gal. 4:5; Rom. 3:24; Heb. 9:12, 15; John 8:34, 36). So far as the atoning death of Christ is concerned, redemption has already been completed once for all (Heb. 9:26), but it must be received on the basis of faith by each person in his own day (Rom. 1:16-17). At the same time we must remember that Christ died for the Church as well as for each believer (Eph. 5:25). While the Church is composed of the *redeemed*, it is called to be a *redeeming* society through its ministry in the name of the Redeemer.

God is King and his people are his servants. His kingship is exercised through the Messiah, Jesus, who is also Servant. Like our Lord we are called to a ministry of the compassionate deed, the spoken word, and the dedicated life. We do not have his miraculous power, but we have channels through which his power still operates in meeting the needs of men. He works through doctors, nurses, medicines, hospitals, loved ones, friends, pastors, prayer—through the Church on the mission field and at home. We cannot atone for sin, but we can lead people to the One who has made atonement. We are instruments in his hand for feeding the hungry and ministering to the whole man in the total community. We are Christ's witnesses in preaching and teaching the gospel of the Kingdom. We seek to evangelize the nonbeliever and to build up the believer in Christian faith and life. We help men to find their vocation under God as good stewards of his manifold grace. As we give our lives into his hands, his love flows through us into the lives of others.

God is Father and his people are his children. It is through the Son of God that we become the sons of God. This is the doctrine of regeneration or the new birth set forth so clearly in the Gospel of John (1:13; 3:1-21). Men are always born into a family relationship, not in isolation. We are born of the Spirit into the family of God. This means that we have new life, and this new life is received by faith: "For God loved the world so very much that he gave his only unique Son, that whosoever has faith in him should not perish but have eternal life" (the writer's translation of John 3:16). Many people are living in insecurity, sin, and misery because they are outside the family (Luke 15:11-32). It is our privilege to invite them to become members of the family by committing themselves to the Son as Savior and Lord.

Christ is the Head and the Church is his Body or Bride (Eph. 1:23; 5:21-32; Col. 1:18; compare Rev. 21:2). This is Paul's way of expressing the husband-wife relationship found in the Old Testament. Christ loved the Church and gave himself for her. As Head, Christ exercises authority and love; as Body, the Church exercises devotion and reverence. Each member of the Body has a particular task to perform in order for the Body to function as the unity it is (I Cor. 12:12-31; Rom. 12; Eph. 4). If all the human body were any one organ, the body would be a monstrosity. Its unity and usefulness come through the diversity of gifts, and it is the responsibility of each person to find the place in which he can best serve through the Church. Once a person has accepted Jesus Christ as Savior and Lord, he has opened his life to the will of God. This means he seeks God's will in the choice of a vocation and in the execution of that vocation. He seeks to follow the leading of the Spirit as a good steward of God's manifold grace, especially as a steward of the gospel of grace. As members of the Body, we must face the fact that Christ has broken down "the dividing wall of hostility" between Jew and Gentile (Eph. 2:14). In the Church "there cannot be Greek and Jew, circumcised and uncircumcised, barbarian, Scythian, slave, free man, but Christ is all, and in all" (Col. 3:11; compare Gal. 3:28). As the Body of Christ the Church is the community of the resurrected Messiah, called to do what Christ did in the body. In the Lord's Supper, Christians bind themselves anew to him and to one another as members of his mystical Body.

God is the Vinedresser, Christ the Vine, and the disciples the branches (John 15:1-11). Under the Old Covenant Israel was the Vine, but because she so often failed God she suffered under the judgment of God. Under the New Covenant Jesus is the true Vine, and God is the Vinedresser who removes the unfruitful branches and prunes the good branches to make them more fruitful. But the branches can bear fruit only as they abide in the Vine.

God is glorified in the disciples' fruit-bearing. Christ's purpose in
speaking of this relationship to his disciples is that they may know
his joy.

God is Shepherd and his people are the sheep (Luke 12:32; 15:
3-7). He is concerned for the whole flock and for every sheep in
it (see Ps. 23). The kings of Israel were supposed to be shepherds
of their people, but most of them preyed upon the sheep. The New
David would be the true Shepherd of the sheep. The Shepherd
God became incarnate in Jesus, who throughout his ministry
showed a Shepherd's care for his people. In John 10:11 he says,
"I am the good shepherd. The good shepherd lays down his life
for the sheep." At the same time he is "the Lamb of God, who
takes away the sin of the world" (John 1:29). When the seer on
Patmos looked for the Lion of the tribe of Judah to open the
scroll of destiny, he did not see a lion but "a Lamb standing, as
though it had been slain" (Rev. 5:5-6). The mighty power of God
is not that of a ravaging lion but that of a Lamb slain. Then we
read:

> For the Lamb in the midst of the throne will be their shep-
>   herd,
> and he will guide them to springs of living water;
> and God will wipe away every tear from their eyes
>
> (Rev. 7:17).

The Lamb is the Shepherd. Who better than the Lamb, that has
endured the Cross, is qualified to sit in the midst of the throne
of heaven? We are in his care forever.

The Holy Spirit Works in the People of God

God has revealed himself as Father, Son, and Holy Spirit (Matt.
28:19; II Cor. 13:14; Eph. 1:3-14). The Old Testament has much
to say of the work of the Spirit of God in nature and in man,
although he is not presented in as sharply personal terms as in the
New Testament. Through his Spirit, God inspired the prophets,
endowed various leaders with power and wisdom, and generated
godly character. It was prophesied that the Spirit of the Lord
would rest upon the Messiah (Isa. 11:2; compare 61:1) and be
poured out upon God's people (Isa. 44:3) to give them a new
heart (Ezek. 36:26-27). It was also foretold that the Spirit would
be poured out on all flesh (Joel 2:28-32; Acts 2:16-21).

In the New Testament considerable attention is given to the

work of the Spirit in relation to the person and work of Jesus in the days of his flesh. However, the Spirit was to come as Counselor in a special way after Jesus' earthly life had been completed (Luke 24:49; John 7:37-39; 14:25-26; 15:26; 16:7-14; Acts 1:8): to minister to his disciples by empowering them, teaching them all things, bringing Jesus' teachings to their remembrance, bearing witness to Christ, guiding them into all truth, and declaring the things that are to come; and to minister to the world by convincing it of sin, righteousness, and judgment.

The Book of Acts records the fulfillment of the promise. The Holy Spirit came in power at Pentecost and has continued his creative and redemptive work through the centuries. In Acts, Luke presents Christianity as the true Judaism and the Church as the instrument through which the Holy Spirit carries on the mighty works of the Kingdom which Jesus began to do (Acts 1:1). The gospel is carried to Rome, the capital of the empire, and is on its way "to the end of the earth." The Holy Spirit is the Christian's guide, the baptizer, the source of witnessing, the inspirer of Scripture writers, the punisher of evildoers, and the Counselor.

According to the letters of the New Testament the Holy Spirit is the source of the life of the people of God. These letters are addressed to congregations and leaders in the Church, not to persons separated from the Church. They concentrate on the message of salvation, which is the doctrine of the Christian life. Salvation is the Kingdom of God in the Synoptic Gospels, eternal life in John, fellowship with God in Hebrews, and the righteousness of God in Paul. These are not different salvations but different ways of expressing God's work through Christ in our behalf. Since Paul wrote more of the New Testament letters than anyone else, his terminology will be used here most often, though much of what he says is paralleled by other writers.

Throughout the centuries many Christians have recognized from their study of the Scriptures three tenses of salvation in Christian experience: past (justification), present progressive (sanctification), and future (glorification). There is, first of all, the *past tense* of salvation. Christ made atonement for sin once for all, and those who have accepted him as Savior and Lord have been saved and stand in a status of salvation. "For by grace you have been saved through faith; and this is not your own doing, it is the gift of God—not because of works, lest any man should boast" (Eph. 2:8-9). Salvation is received through faith as dynamic commitment to Christ. To commit oneself to Christ as Savior means to say to him in all sincerity: "I accept you as the One who can do for me what I cannot do for myself in forgiving my sin, in relating me rightly to God, to my neighbor, and to my innermost being." To commit oneself to him as Lord means to say to him in all sincerity: "I accept you as the Commander-in-chief of my life. You give the orders, and by the grace of God I will obey in so far as I know your will and can learn it." This faith is the gift of God, for "no one can say 'Jesus is Lord' except by the Holy Spirit" (I Cor. 12:3; compare Rom. 10:9). John also makes clear the dynamic nature of saving faith (John 3:16) and the reality of salvation in the past tense (I John 3:14; compare I Peter 2:9; Heb. 4:2).

Salvation in the past tense is described by several terms: justification, reconciliation, redemption, forgiveness, and adoption. Justification reveals God's righteousness as gracious (Rom. 3:21-26). It is the act of God as Judge in removing the criminal (sinner) from the category of the condemned and placing him in the category of the acquitted on the basis of faith in Jesus Christ. "Therefore, since we are justified by faith, we have peace with God through our Lord Jesus Christ" (Rom. 5:1; see also 1:17; Gal. 3:11; I Cor. 6:11). In reconciliation the person who is estranged from God on account of sin, becomes the friend of God through Christ (Rom. 5:11). Furthermore, to those who are reconciled, God has committed the ministry and message of reconciliation (II Cor. 5:17-21). Redemption is God's act in freeing the slave (sinner) from the bondage to sin, to the wrath of God, to the law, and to death (Rom. 3:24; 6:1-23; 5:1—8:39). To be free from bondage to the law does not mean that the law is evil or that a Christian can be a libertine. It means that a Christian is freed from trying to save himself by legalism, freed from the condemnation of the law, and freed to live as a child of God. Forgiveness is not confined to the time of justification. Adoption is God's bringing the redeemed sinner into the family of the redeemed (Gal. 4:4-5). These five words (justification, reconciliation, redemption, forgiveness, and adoption) are not five different salvations but five ways of expressing the believer's entrance into God's abundance.

Justification is the beginning of a pilgrimage, not the end of the road. The Christian not only says, "I have been saved," but also, "I am being saved." Paul states the *present tense* of salvation as a process in these words: "For the word of the cross is folly to those who are perishing, but to us who are being saved it is the power of God" (I Cor. 1:18; compare 15:2; I John 5:12). Paul had been converted on the Damascus Road—that is, he had been justified—but in this passage he numbers himself among those who "are being saved." These doctrines of salvation are not contradictory but complementary. Paul was already a redeemed child of God, but he was also in the process of becoming the child God purposed him to be. He frankly admitted that he had not attained perfection but was pressing on toward the goal (Phil. 3:12-16). The baby in your home may be your child biologically, legally, in the eyes of men, and in the eyes of God; yet he will be more your child in spirit and in truth after he has lived under your guidance and love. We are children of God, yet we are in the process of becoming the children we ought to be under the tutelage of the Holy Spirit.

The words "sanctify" and "sanctification" come to mind when one is thinking of the Christian life. These words come from the root meaning "to be holy"; therefore, sanctification is a making holy or separating unto God. Sometimes it is regarded as a gift of God in past time, simultaneous with justification but not a "second blessing" (I Cor. 1:2; 6:11; Heb. 10:29). By justification a person is set free; by sanctification he is given the status of a saint, bound to the Holy God and his people. Sanctification, however, looks to the future for completion (I Thess. 4:3; II Cor. 7:1; Rom. 6:19). The saint is to become increasingly in practice what he already is in status and relationship.

Christian ethical behavior rests upon what God has done, follows the pattern of the life of Christ, and finds its dynamic in the Holy Spirit. What God has done is basic to the entire message of the Bible. After Paul has set forth God's saving work in Romans 1-11, he says, "I appeal to you therefore, brethren, by the mercies of God, to present your bodies as a living sacrifice, holy and acceptable to God, which is your spiritual worship" (12:1). In response to what God has done, Christians, in deep gratitude, are to offer their lives to him in a service that is also worship (compare Eph. 4:1). Christian ethics is rooted in Christian faith and in the willingness to do God's will (John 7:17).

The disciples are to follow the Master's dedication to the Father's will in humility and service. In commending the grace of generosity to the Corinthians, Paul tells them of the generosity of

Christ: "For you know the grace of our Lord Jesus Christ, that though he was rich, yet for your sake he became poor, so that by his poverty you might become rich" (II Cor. 8:9). In Romans 15:3 he calls to mind Christ's unselfishness, and in Philippians 2:5-8 his self-giving.

The Holy Spirit is the author of the Christian life from beginning to end (Rom. 8; Gal. 5:16-25; I Cor. 3:16-17; 6:19; II Cor. 3:17). As an illustration of the ethical dynamic of the Spirit, Paul says: "The fruit of the Spirit is love, joy, peace, patience, kindness, goodness, faithfulness, gentleness, self-control" (Gal. 5:22-23; compare Rom. 5:5; Eph. 4:25-32). It is no accident that love heads this list, for "God shows his love for us in that while we were yet sinners Christ died for us" (Rom. 5:8). Or as John tells us, "God is love" (I John 4:16) and "We love, because he first loved us" (I John 4:19). Such love is self-giving. The Christian puts love into action in response to the love of God and the operation of the Holy Spirit (Rom. 5:5). This love is to operate in all areas of life: in the Church fellowship (Rom. 12:9-13; I Cor. 12-13; Rom. 14:21; John 15:12; I John 4:20); in relation to all men, including, by implication, the political state (Rom. 12:14-21; 13:8-10 and 1-7; I Peter 2:13-17; Mark 12:17; Acts 5:29); and in the Christian household (Col. 3:18—4:1; Eph. 5:1-2; 5:21—6:9; Philemon; I Peter 2:18—3:8). It is impossible to love God without loving one's brother also (I John 4:20; compare John 15:12). The Christian is to put no stumbling block in a brother's way (Rom. 14:13-23).

Just as faith is essential to the beginning of the Christian life, so it is throughout the Christian life. The Christian's commitment to Christ must be renewed time and time again. Faith issues in faithfulness and hope (Heb. 11:1). According to the Letter of James, faith expresses itself in doing the word, bridling the tongue, showing no partiality to the rich, loving one's neighbor, avoiding covetousness, exercising patience, telling the truth, visiting the sick and praying for them (especially directed to elders), and leading the sinner back from the error of his way.

As Christians we live by a sure faith, though we struggle with temptation and the forces of evil. God has given us means for moving in the direction of "mature manhood" in Christ (Eph. 4:1-16): the Bible, the sacraments, prayer, corporate worship, Christian homes and friends, Christian publications, visual aids, and opportunities for Christian witness and service—all understood and utilized in the context of the Church as the family of God, in whose life little children have a vital part (Gen. 12:3; 17:1-14; Deut. 6:4-25; Acts 2:39; 16:14-15, 33; I Cor. 7:14). God also enables the Christian to grow through the things which he suffers (John 15:18-20; Rom. 5:3-4; Heb. 12:3-11; II Cor. 12:1-10).

Finally, the Christian says, "I shall be saved." This *future tense* of salvation is inseparably bound up with the past and the present tenses. It is the person who is committed to Christ in faith who will be glorified. In Romans 5:9 Paul says, "Since, therefore, we are now justified by his blood, much more shall we be saved by him from the wrath of God" (compare John 14:19). We are saved from tragedy that is too great for the mind of man fully to comprehend. The wrath of God is not in opposition to the love of God; it is the consequence of rejecting his love. Paul states this future aspect of salvation more positively in these words: "Through him [Christ] we have obtained access to this grace in which we stand, and we rejoice in our hope of sharing the glory of God" (Rom. 5:2).

The Holy Spirit is our guarantee of that "house not made with hands, eternal in the heavens" (II Cor. 5:1-5; compare Eph. 1:13-14; II Cor. 1:22). The hope of the Christian's resurrection rests upon Christ's resurrection. The body "is sown a physical body, it is raised a spiritual body" (I Cor. 15:44). The person in his essential integrity is raised. As in this world we have a medium of identification, communication, and service, so the spiritual body is adapted to the world to come.

The life to come will be a going home to God and his people (John 14:1-7), where the deepest meanings of life are realized. We now live *in* Christ, we shall then live *with* Christ (Phil. 1:23; Rom. 6:8). "It does not yet appear what we shall be, but we know that when he appears we shall be like him" (I John 3:2). God's glorious surprise will transcend all our present imaginings. The individual Christian's salvation is bound up with that of the Church for which Christ died (Eph. 5:25).

The whole work of salvation is in the hands of the sovereign and gracious God. The doctrine of election affirms this (Rom. 8:28-30; 9:1-29; Eph. 1:3-14). Paul longed for his Jewish brethren to accept Christ. In Romans 9:1-29 he insists upon God's sovereignty in salvation, but in the same context (Rom. 9:30—10:21) upon Old Israel's responsibility for rejecting the gospel.

This does not mean that God has rejected his people, for there is a Remnant. One day Old Israel will become one with the New Israel in Christ (Rom. 11:26). Though man's responsibility is by no means the equivalent of God's sovereignty, it is real, for God does not place him in the category of an animal or thing. The biblical writers nowhere attempt to harmonize God's sovereignty and man's freedom. The human brain is too small to solve so great a mystery, and it is the part of humility and wisdom to leave the matter where Paul left it: "O the depth of the riches and wisdom and knowledge of God! How unsearchable are his judgments and how inscrutable his ways!" (Rom. 11:33).

Mankind

The hourglass expands in its movement from the Church to mankind. Throughout all that has been said about the Church, it has been apparent that it has a mission to the world. Israel had such a mission, and the Church as the New Israel also has a mission. This mission includes evangelism, Christian education, warning, healing, and the life of love in action.

Jesus saw men in need of compassion and redemption (Matt. 9:35-38). He regarded a man's life as valuable to the man himself (Mark 8:34-37). In Jesus' eyes persons are of great value. God takes care of the birds, and you are of more value than birds; he will take care of you (Matt. 6:25-33). "Even the hairs of your head are all numbered" (Matt. 10:30). In Jesus' day sheep often represented commercial value. He said, "Of how much more value is a man than a sheep!" (Matt. 12:12). In other words, human beings take precedence over property. They are also of more value than institutions, even than the Sabbath (Matt. 12:9-14). "The sabbath was made for man, not man for the sabbath" (Mark 2:27). Even tax collectors and sinners, people in the lowest social stratum of his day, were the objects of Jesus' love. The shepherd leaves the ninety-nine to search for the sheep that is lost (Luke 15:3-7).

To Jesus, sin was primarily a matter of inner spirit (Mark 7:20-23). He dealt more tenderly with those guilty of sexual immorality than with the self-righteous. Sin places men in the category of the lost, and Jesus "came to seek and to save the lost" (Luke 19:10). Sin is giving first place to anything less than the Kingdom (Matt. 19:16-22; compare Luke 12:13-21). It is neglecting to use the talents which are God's blessing (Matt. 25:14-30). It is forfeiting one's sonship to God (Luke 15:11-32). It is social as well as personal (Matt. 11:20-24).

In his letters Paul stresses the fact that every man, Jew or Gentile, is unrighteous and cannot save himself. Sin is racial (that is, a matter concerning the entire human race) as well as personal. Sin came into the world through the first Adam and death came through sin, "and so death spread to all men because all men sinned" (Rom. 5:12-21). Christ is the last Adam (I Cor. 15:45). "For as in Adam all die, so also in Christ shall all be made alive" (I Cor. 15:22). All men were in Adam as father of the human race and are therefore the extension of Adam—just as the Old Testament writers thought of all Israelites as being in Jacob and becoming the extension of Jacob. To be in Adam is to be in the realm of sin and death; but to be in Christ, the last Adam, is to be in the realm of justification and life. The Church as the Body of Christ is the New Race in which worldly distinctions are abolished. It is the creation of God by redemption. To be in Christ is to be a new creation (Gal. 6:15; II Cor. 5:17; Col. 3:9-11). The image of God is being renewed in the Christian (Col. 3:10). Adam was grasping and wanted to be like God (Gen. 3), and every succeeding Adam except One has followed in the first Adam's footsteps. Christ, the last Adam, was not grasping "but emptied himself, taking the form of a servant" (Phil. 2:5-11).

John presents the problem of sin and the remedy for sin in strong contrasts:

The World ..	John 15:18-19; 18:36; I John 2:15	The Kingdom
Unbelief ...	John 3:16-18; 6:64; I John 5:12	Faith
Bondage ...	John 8:31-38	Freedom
Darkness ...	John 1:5; 8:12; I John 1:5; 2:9 .	Light
Death	John 5:24; 3:16	Eternal Life
Hate and Fear	John 15:18-19; I John 4:18-20 ..	Love
Lawlessness .	I John 3:4-6	Abiding in God

In the Letter to the Hebrews sin is unbelief, stubbornness, or hardening of the heart (3:1-19). It is neglect of "such a great salvation" (2:3). In James it is yielding to temptation, laziness, omission of doing good, and indifference to the needs of others. In Jude it is active hostility to God. The most generally used word for sin in both Testaments means "to miss the mark." Regardless of what words are used to designate sin, it is always a missing of the mark which God has set for us. Any thought, word, deed, attitude, or feeling contrary to the Spirit of Christ is sin.

In the light of the Cross sin is that which puts to death the Best that God himself can do. The doctrine of demons and the doctrine of racial sin are never used anywhere in the New Testament to excuse man from his responsibility. These doctrines confront us with the tragedy of our predicament and our need of God's salvation. Apart from Christ we are lost sinners, but through Christ we may become redeemed saints, members of the family of God.

The New Creation

The Bible begins with creation and ends with the New Creation. However, between beginning and end, considerable attention is given to the hope of the people of God. The Old Testament prophets looked forward to a new David, a new Covenant, a new heart, a new life, a new Jerusalem, and a new creation.

The New Testament records the fulfillment of the promise. The Kingdom began to dawn in Jesus' person and work. He was the New David, and he established the New Covenant. The work of the Holy Spirit is Kingdom work. Eternal life is the new life generated by the Holy Spirit in the new birth. Persons in Christ are already new creations. They have been raised from the death of sin and walk in newness of life. The gospel is good news centering in what God has done through Christ.

The promise has been fulfilled but it has not been consummated. The Kingdom has come and it is yet to come. The day of peace for which the prophets longed (Isa. 2:1-4; Micah 4:1-4) is yet to be.

Jesus' statements concerning the Son of Man anticipate the consummation of the Kingdom (Mark 8:38; 13:35; 14:62). We still pray the prayer he taught his early disciples:

> "Thy kingdom come,
> Thy will be done,
> On earth as it is in heaven."

The Apostles included the return of Christ as Savior and Judge in their earliest preaching of the gospel (Acts 3:20; 10:42). Paul deals with the Second Coming in I and II Thessalonians and returns to it from time to time in his other letters (for example, Phil. 3:20). The resurrection of the dead is associated with the consummation of the Kingdom. The completion of the individual's salvation is bound up with God's purpose for the Church and the universe. Paul understands the whole creation to be "groaning in travail together until now" (Rom. 8:18-25). Somehow the created universe seems to be included in God's redemptive purpose. In the Letter to the Hebrews considerable stress is laid on heaven as the consummation of salvation (11:10, 16; 12:22; 13:14), but this does not invalidate the expectation of Christ's Second Coming (9:28; 10:25). Even in the Gospel of John, which concentrates upon eternal life as a present reality, the final resurrection is yet to come (5:28-29; 6:44; 12:48). By the time II Peter was written, some Christians were wondering why the Day of the Lord had not come, and the author tells them that "with the Lord one day is as a thousand years" (3:8). He also maintains the certainty of the New Creation: "But according to his promise we wait for new heavens and a new earth in which righteousness dwells" (3:13). Unfortunately many people have abused the doctrine of the Second Coming by claiming to know the unknowable and by neglecting the application of the ethics of Jesus to certain aspects of life in the here and now. Others have simply ignored the doctrine. Just as the first coming of Jesus enriched the prophecy which anticipated him, so his Second Coming will exceed and enrich all our expectations.

It is appropriate that the Book of Revelation closes the Canon. In it the seer on Patmos has a vision of the New Jerusalem. The book seems to have been written against the background of the persecution of Christians under the Roman Emperor Domitian (A.D. 81-96). Christians would not submit to the demand that they worship the emperor. This refusal sometimes meant martyrdom. John commends some of the churches in Asia Minor and rebukes others. He issues a summons to repentance and steadfast loyalty to Christ in the midst of trial. Every person will belong either to the beast or to the Lamb, but in the final analysis the victory will belong to God and his people. This victory includes the triumph over cosmic evil (devil, demons, etc.; see Heb. 2:14).

With John we see the vision of the New Jerusalem (Rev. 21:1 —22:5). There will be a new heaven and a new earth. The New Jerusalem in one sense is the Church as the Bride of Christ. It stands for God's dwelling with his people, for the end of sin, weeping, pain, and death. It stands for all the creative work of God brought to its consummation. The eternal city is built upon historical foundations: on its gates are inscribed the names of the twelve tribes of Israel and on the foundations of its walls the names of the twelve Apostles of the Lamb.

Things such as gold, glass, and precious stones are to be used as instruments of the city of God, but in the final analysis the city is in the realm of the Spirit, for in it there will be no need for a temple—"its temple is the Lord God the Almighty and the Lamb," and the glory of God is its light. Nations shall walk by the light of the city and kings shall bring their glory into it, reminding us that God's salvation is national and social as well as personal.

The Bible begins with the story of man in a garden and ends with the story of man in a city, but the city is a "garden city"; and in this garden city there is a river of the water of life and the tree of life. That from which the flaming cherubs barred sinful man (Gen. 3:24) is now made available forever. The leaves of the tree are for the healing of the nations.

Is this a symbol of heaven or of earth? It is a symbol of both, as the eternal redeems the temporal. For those in whose heart is the New Jerusalem and whose heart is in the New Jerusalem, the song of the redeemed is already a reality, but one day that song will be sung without a single discordant note. Like the Old Testament, the New Testament ends on a note of hope and expectation. God who has acted mightily in history, and supremely in Christ, will through that same Christ accomplish the New Creation.

Conclusion

The story of salvation as set forth in the Bible from creation to Christ and on to the New Creation speaks of privilege and responsibility. There is nothing really like it. Parts of it were recorded at different times over more than a millennium. It was written in two major languages and a multitude of literary forms. Some writers did not know what other writers were writing or had written. Yet together their various contributions tell one story. In this story we find our true security, for it is God's story. "The grass withers, the flower fades; but the word of our God will stand for ever" (Isa. 40:8). God's salvation places upon us as the people of God a corresponding responsibility. For "to whom much is given, of him will much be required" (Luke 12:48). But the requirement of sharing the story is itself a joyous privilege.

HOW WE GOT THE BIBLE

One of the most interesting and thrilling chapters in the history of the Church is the story of the transmission of the Holy Scriptures. From the time when they were first written and throughout subsequent centuries when they were translated into more than a thousand languages, the transmission of the Scriptures has been both an evidence for and the result of God's providential care. Alphabets were invented and languages reduced to writing in order to convey the divine oracles to nations hitherto illiterate.

To take several examples, Ulfilas, the first bishop of the Goths in the fourth century, Mesrop, the missionary to the Armenians in the fifth century, and Cyril and Methodius, the apostles to the Slavs in the ninth century, are honored for having created the possibility of literature for millions of people. On the other hand, martyrdom was sometimes the price paid for daring to render the Bible into the language of the ordinary people, as when William Tyndale, an exile from his native England, was hunted out in Belgium, arrested on charges of heresy, and first strangled and then burnt in the prison yard of Vilvoorden, near Brussels.

Other deeds of heroism, though less well known, are no less stirring. The first translation of part of the Old Testament into Manx, the Celtic dialect spoken on the Isle of Man, was saved as John Kelly, when shipwrecked, held the manuscript above the water for five hours before being rescued. The Herculean labors of missionary translators, working incessantly and sometimes in the face of grave disabilities, are a tribute to Christian perseverance. Thus, the former English shoemaker, William Carey, at the time of his death in 1834 had translated the Bible, in whole or in part, either alone or with others, into twenty-six languages of India. Somewhat similar was the work of Samuel I. J. Schereschewsky, a brilliant Lithuanian Jew who, having been converted to Christianity, went as a missionary to China. Despite a paralytic affliction that kept him in a wheel chair for twenty-one years, during which time he could move only the muscles of one hand and arm, he translated the entire Bible into a Chinese language called Easy Wenli (which is a colloquial form of Mandarin). This version has been called "The One-Finger Bible," because the translator had to type out the entire manuscript using only one finger. Such examples of Christian determination to translate and transmit the Word of God are only a few from many that illuminate the annals of Church history.

The Making of Ancient Books

Before giving the principal stages of the transmission of the Bible, it is necessary to describe briefly the materials and methods of ancient scribes. Until the invention of printing with movable type about the middle of the fifteenth century, the surviving works of all ancient authors had to be passed on in handwritten copies (the word "manuscript" comes from two Latin words, *manu* and *scriptum,* meaning "written by hand").

The two materials most widely used for the making of books in antiquity were papyrus and parchment. Papyrus is an aquatic plant of the sedge family which grew abundantly in the marshy lands of Egypt in the vicinity of the Delta. When mature the plant, which resembles a stalk of corn, was cut down and the stem divided into sections about a foot in length. Each of these was split open and the core of pith removed. After the pith was sliced into thin strips, these tapelike pieces were placed side by side on a flat surface, and another layer laid crosswise on top. As the two layers were pressed and pounded together, a sheet of papyrus was produced that was remarkably durable.

Even more durable as writing material was parchment. This was made from the skins of antelopes, sheep, calves, and other animals. The younger the animal, the finer was the quality of the skin. Vellum was the finest quality of extra-thin parchment, sometimes secured from animals not yet born. After the hair had been removed and the surface dressed, such a sheet was lined by scores made with a blunt-pointed instrument drawn along a rule. In the case of the papyrus sheet, one side was already "ruled" because of the direction of the fibers in the strips of pith.

There were two main forms for ancient books. The older form was the scroll. This was made by sewing or gluing sheets of papyrus or parchment together until a long strip was secured. The ends were then attached to two dowels of wood, bone, or metal. The maximum average length of such a scroll was about thirty or thirty-two feet; anything longer became excessively unwieldy to handle. The writing was placed in narrow columns, each two or three inches wide, running at right angles to the length of the scroll. Usually only one side of the scroll was utilized.

The other common form of book in antiquity was the codex, or "leaf book." This was made from either parchment or papyrus in a format resembling modern books. A certain number of sheets were stacked on top of one another and folded down the middle. Depending upon the size of book desired, one or more of such quires, as they were called, would be fastened together at the back. There was an art connected with the manufacture of such parchment codices. Since the hair side of parchment was darker in color than the flesh side, the aesthetically minded scribe was careful to place the sheets in such a way that wherever the codex was opened the flesh side of one sheet would face the flesh side of another sheet, and the hair side face hair side. Unlike the scroll, the codex could conveniently receive writing on both sides of each sheet. Depending upon the dimensions of the codex, one, two, or even occasionally three or four columns of script were placed on each page. The magnificent Codex Sinaiticus, a manuscript of the Greek Bible dating from the fourth century A.D., presents a sumptuous appearance with eight narrow columns of writing on two pages wherever the codex is opened.

It is obvious that the advantages of the codex form of book greatly outweighed those of the scroll. The Church soon found that economy of production (since both sides of the page were utilized) and ease of consulting passages (no need to unroll long portions of a scroll in hunting for a desired passage) made it advisable to adopt the codex rather than the scroll for its sacred books. It may be, also, that the desire to differentiate the external form of the Christian Bible from the Jewish scrolls of the synagogue was a motivating factor in the change from scrolls to codices.

The inks which were used for papyrus and parchment were necessarily different. In the case of papyrus a carbon-base ink, made from soot, gum, and water, was usually employed. This kind of ink did not stick well to parchment, and so another kind of ink was made of gall nuts. Sulphate of iron was afterwards added to it, as were other chemicals which produced a wide variety of colors. Titles were often written with vermilion ink, and today we still speak of the "rubrics" of a literary work (from the Latin word *ruber,* meaning "red") and of "red-letter" days (which were marked on the calendar in vermilion).

Sometimes the parchment of a codex was used a second time. Particularly in times of economic depression, an older, worn-out volume would be salvaged and reused for another literary work after the former writing had been scraped or washed off. Such a manuscript is called a palimpsest ("re-scraped"). Today, by the use of chemical reagents and ultraviolet ray lamps it is possible to decipher the almost totally obliterated underwriting of palimpsest manuscripts. An important palimpsest of the Scriptures is the fifth-century copy of the Greek Bible known as the Codex Ephraemi, which in the twelfth century was erased in order to receive the homilies of the Syrian Church Father, Ephraem. (This is, unfortunately, not the only instance when sermons have covered over the Scripture text!)

Two modes of producing manuscripts were in common use in antiquity. One was the way of copying. An individual would make a new copy, word by word and letter by letter, from an exemplar of the literary work desired. It was inevitable (as anyone can see for himself who tries to copy an extended document) that accidental changes would be introduced into the text. The accuracy of the new copy would, of course, depend upon the degree of the copyist's familiarity with the language and content of what he was transcribing, as well as upon the care he exercised in performing his task. Furthermore, the likelihood that errors would creep into the work of the scribe was compounded by certain features of ancient writing. Several letters in both the Hebrew and the Greek alphabets were similar, and were likely to be confused even by the most conscientious scribe. Moreover, the fact that ordinarily no space was left between words and between sentences made for more than one type of mistake.

The other mode of producing a book was that employed at a scriptorium. Here a reader, or lector, would read aloud, slowly and distinctly, from the exemplar while several scribes seated about him would write, producing simultaneously as many new copies as there were scribes at work. This dictation method, however, multiplied the kinds of errors that crept into the text. In addition to those occasioned by the inattentiveness of the scribe or their unfamiliarity with the material, there were others which arose from the circumstance that certain letters and words in Greek came to be pronounced alike (as in English the words "grate" and "great," and "their" and "there"). For example, in later Greek the words for "we" and "you" and for "us" and "you" were indistinguishable to the ear. Consequently, in the epistles of the New Testament, it is often difficult or impossible to decide on the basis of manuscript evidence which forms were originally used. It should be added that among the Jews very great care was taken to copy the Old Testament with exactness, and the dictation method was seldom employed. On the other hand, owing to the rapid expansion of the Christian Church and the consequent demand for many copies of the Scriptures, sometimes the speedy multiplication of copies, particularly by nonprofessional scribes, seemed to be of greater importance than strict accuracy of detail.

In addition to divergencies of text arising from inadvertence, at times other alterations were deliberately introduced into the sacred text. Thus, a more highly developed liturgy in the Church and the development of ascetical practices in monastic communities led occasionally to the modification of what had been previously transmitted. For example, in the oldest manuscripts of the Gospel of Matthew the Lord's Prayer (Matt. 6:9-13) closes with the words, "And lead us not into temptation, But deliver us from evil." It is only in the later manuscripts that we find a liturgically appropriate doxology added at the end. At first this was twofold in form ("For thine is the power and the glory forever") and later threefold ("For thine is the kingdom and the power and the glory, forever. Amen"). Although Roman Catholics end the prayer with "deliver us from evil," most Protestants will agree that this later doxology is an eminently appropriate conclusion to the prayer which our Lord taught his followers.

Among ascetical corruptions which have crept into the text during the course of its transmission is the addition in later manuscripts of a reference to fasting in such passages as Mark 9:29; Acts 10:30; and I Corinthians 7:5. (The King James Version, which translates the later, corrupted form of Greek text, can be compared here with the Revised Standard Version, which returns to the earliest form of Greek text.) Again, sometimes the copyist succumbed to the natural desire to fill out one account with material from a parallel account. Thus, in Colossians 1:14 only the later and more corrupt manuscripts have the words "through his blood," which some well-meaning scribe introduced into this verse from the parallel expression in Ephesians 1:7.

It should be observed that, although there are thousands of divergencies of text in the manuscripts of the Bible (more in the New Testament than in the Old), the great majority of them involve inconsequential details, such as alternative spellings, order of words, and interchange of synonyms. Among the relatively few instances of variants involving the substance of the record, modern scholars are usually able to determine with more or less probability what the original text was.

The Earliest Manuscripts of the
Old and New Testaments

Parts of the Bible were transmitted in written form from the outset; as, for example, certain law codes in the Old Testament and all of the letters in the New Testament. On the other hand, the content of large sections of both Testaments was passed on from one generation to another by word of mouth before being put in written form. Thus, the stories of the antediluvians and of the patriarchs in Genesis, the narratives of the Exodus and of the wanderings of the Israelites in the wilderness, the sagas in the Book of Judges and the Books of Samuel, these and other similar accounts were probably told and retold for centuries before they were reduced to writing. Furthermore, much of the contents of the prophetical books was at first delivered orally to those to whom the prophets were sent. In the New Testament, the materials bearing on the life and teaching of Jesus Christ were passed on by word of mouth for decades. The first Gospel (that according to Mark) was written sometime at the end of the fifties or during the sixties of the first century; the latest Gospel (that according to John) was published toward the close of the first Christian century. Likewise, the recollection of what had happened at Pentecost and in the earliest stages of Jewish and Gentile evangelism was preserved in the memories of those whom Luke consulted preparatory to writing the Book of Acts.

Once the several books of the Bible had been written, their contents naturally took on a more fixed form. Thereafter it was chiefly through scribal inadvertence that modifications crept into the text.

Until 1947 the earliest known Hebrew manuscript of the Old Testament (except for a few insignificant scraps) was one which dates from the end of the ninth Christian century. The form of Hebrew text contained in this and the later Hebrew manuscripts is the so-called Masoretic recension, or edition, of the Hebrew Bible. This was prepared by Jewish scholars, the Masoretes, in the fifth and sixth centuries A.D., on the basis of copies representing slightly divergent forms of text current in older manuscripts. Beginning in 1947 a series of discoveries of scrolls preserved in caves

at Qumran by the Dead Sea resulted in the acquisition of much
older documents varying in size but covering all the books of the
Old Testament except Esther. These scrolls and fragments of
scrolls date from the centuries just before and after the beginning
of the Christian era. It is noteworthy that in general the text preserved in these scrolls, so far as they have been deciphered at the
time of this writing, agrees with the traditional, Masoretic form of
the Old Testament text.

As regards the New Testament text, literally scores of important early manuscripts have come to light during the past century.
In 1859 the German scholar, Constantine von Tischendorf, discovered in a monastery on Mount Sinai the famous Codex Sinaiticus, a magnificent parchment copy of the Greek Bible, dating
from the fourth century A.D. It is now in the British Museum.
From the late fourth or early fifth century is a parchment codex
of the Four Gospels in Greek, purchased in 1906 by Mr. Charles
L. Freer of Detroit from a dealer in antiquities in Cairo. Today
this manuscript, called the Codex Washingtonianus, is on display
in the Freer Art Museum at the Smithsonian Institution of Wash-
ington, D. C. About 1930 a British collector of antiquities, Mr. A.
Chester Beatty, acquired more than a dozen early Greek codices,
including three fragmentary papyri containing portions of many
of the books of the New Testament. What makes these manuscripts important is the fact that they date from about the third
century. They are now in the Beatty Museum at Dublin. In 1935
a British paleographer, C. H. Roberts, edited a tiny papyrus fragment (measuring only two and one-half by three and one-half
inches), found in a collection at Manchester, which proved to be
what is still the oldest extant portion of the New Testament. It is
thought to date from the first half of the second century, and contains about thirty words from the eighteenth chapter of the Gospel
according to John.

Still more recently the Swiss bibliophile, Martin Bodmer, acquired several papyrus codices of Greek authors, including books
of the New Testament. In 1956 one of these, Papyrus Bodmer II,
was published. It contains, almost completely preserved, the first
fourteen chapters of the Gospel according to John, with fragments
of the remaining chapters, and dates from about A.D. 200.

These examples of early and important Greek manuscripts of
the New Testament are only a few of many that might be mentioned.

The ninth century saw a marked change in the style of Greek script used in making books; instead of capital or block letters, called "uncials," a running or cursive hand called "minuscules" was adopted and adapted by scribes for writing books. It is customary, therefore, to divide Greek manuscripts into two main categories, uncial and minuscule codices. Furthermore, a special form of biblical manuscript came to be prepared. This was the lectionary, or Church reading book, containing passages of the Scripture arranged according to the ecclesiastical calendar and appointed to be read as the lessons in divine services. Strangely enough, although these lectionaries have been known to scholars for centuries, it is only recently that they have begun to receive the attention which they deserve.

Some idea of the enormous number of extant Greek manuscripts of the New Testament may be secured from the following statistics (as of 1958):

Number of papyri 67
Number of parchment codices
    Uncial script 241
    Minuscule script 2,533
    Lectionaries 1,838

In evaluating the significance of this rich store of manuscripts, it should be recalled that the writings of many ancient classical authors have survived in only a few copies, or even in only one. Furthermore, in most cases the earliest of these nonbiblical manuscripts date from the later Middle Ages and thus are separated from the time of the composition of the original work by more than a thousand years.

Ancient Versions of the Bible

Ancient Versions Made for the Use of Jews

During the fourth and third centuries B.C. more and more Jews, particularly those living in the lands outside of Palestine, lost facility in the use of Hebrew. In order to convey to these people the content of the Old Testament, translations were made from Hebrew into other languages. Beginning about 280 B.C. the first five books of the Old Testament (the Pentateuch) were translated into Greek at Alexandria in Egypt, where there was a large Greek-speaking population of both Jews and Gentiles. In subsequent years the other books of the Old Testament were also rendered into Greek, and this translation, which came to be called the Septuagint (from the legend that it had been made by seventy translators), circulated far and wide. Most of the authors of the New Testament usually quote the Old Testament not from the original Hebrew but from this Old Greek version.

During the centuries just preceding the Christian era, many of the Jews who lived in Palestine felt more at home using Aramaic than Hebrew. (Aramaic is a Semitic language related to Hebrew somewhat as Spanish is related to Portuguese or Dutch to German.) The custom arose of having an interpreter give an Aramaic paraphrase at the reading of the Hebrew Scriptures during the synagogue services. At first the form of these oral paraphrases in Aramaic was more or less fluid, but as time went on, different traditions became fixed and were subsequently reduced to writing. Thus arose the several Aramaic Targums, as they are called, of the Old Testament.

Ancient Versions Intended Chiefly for Christians

Although Jesus and his Apostles customarily spoke Aramaic, which was the mother tongue of most Palestinian Jews of that day, the four inspired records of his life and teachings, as well as the other books of the New Testament, were composed in Greek, which was the language of international culture in the Mediterranean world at that period. Soon, however, the message of the gospel was taken by evangelists and missionaries to people who, though perhaps they knew some Greek, felt more at home using their mother tongue. Thus it came about that during the second century portions of the New Testament were translated for missionary purposes into Syriac and into Latin, and during the third century into Coptic.

One of the oldest forms of the Gospels in Syriac was the so-called Diatessaron. This was a single narrative of the Four Gospels, prepared about A.D. 170 by an Eastern Christian named Tatian. Several rather colloquial renderings of the separate Greek Gospels into Syriac, made about A.D. 200, gave way at the end of the fourth century to a more polished translation called the Peshitta version (the word *Peshitta* means "simple" or "common"). It is still used by Syriac-speaking Christians. The Old Testament in this version probably depends on Targums prepared by Jews or Jewish Christians in Aramaic or Syriac, which are related Semitic dialects. The Peshitta version of the New Testament contains only twenty-two books, omitting II Peter, II and III John, Jude, and Revelation. During the sixth century other Syriac versions were made, containing all twenty-seven books of the New Testament.

Because the Coptic language existed in different dialects along the Nile, several Coptic versions were made at various places and at different times during the third and following centuries. The most important of these are the Sahidic and the Bohairic versions, belonging respectively to Upper (southern) Egypt and Lower (northern) Egypt.

During the fourth century the New Testament and most of the Old Testament were rendered into Gothic by Ulfilas, the first Bishop of the Goths. This version is of interest because its surviving fragments constitute the oldest known remains of any Teutonic language. In the fourth and fifth centuries Christianity was carried to Armenia and Caucasian Georgia, and there also translations of the Scriptures soon became necessary. Similarly the evangelization of Ethiopia, Nubia, Sogdiana, Arabia, and Bulgaria was followed in each case by translations of part or all of the Scriptures.

As was mentioned above, the Latin versions were among the earliest which Christian missionaries prepared. Because of their importance in the transmission of the Bible to the majority of the people of Europe, the history of the Old Latin versions and of Jerome's Latin Vulgate will be given in fuller detail than was necessary in the case of other versions.

The first attempts at translation of the Bible into Latin were rough and literalistic. Some were interlinear versions, with the order of words mechanically conformed to the Greek order. Apparently many separate translations were produced. At the close of the fourth century Jerome complained that there were almost as many variant translations into Latin as there were separate manuscripts. One of the reasons for the diversity, as Augustine said, was that "in the early days of the faith, every man who happened to gain possession of a Greek manuscript and who imagined he had any facility in both languages, however slight that might be, dared to make a translation" (*de doctrina Christiana,* II, xi, 16). Confronted with such a welter of diverse Latin renderings, toward the close of the fourth Christian century, Damasus, the Bishop of Rome, requested Jerome, who was the outstanding biblical scholar of his time, to make a standard Latin version for the use of the Western Churches. This version, the Latin Vulgate, has become the official text of the Roman Catholic Church.

Jerome tells us how he proceeded in his task. On the basis of a comparison of early Greek manuscripts current in his day, he revised that form of the Old Latin text which had become the most familiar in the churches. But on the whole, he says, "I have used my pen with some restraint, and while I have corrected only such passages as seemed to convey a different meaning, I have allowed the rest to remain as they are" (Preface to the Four Gospels).

Jerome's scholarly labors to supply a more accurate biblical text met with indifference and even hostility on the part of the churches. He had, indeed, anticipated in some measure what the reaction to his labors would be. In his Preface to the Four Gospels he asks, "Is there a man, learned or unlearned, who will not, when he takes the volume [of my revision] into his hands, and perceives that what he reads does not suit his settled tastes, break out immediately into violent language, and call me a forger and a profane person for having the audacity to add anything to the ancient books, or to make any changes or corrections therein?" As has happened more than once in subsequent ages, congregations usually preferred a familiar though corrupted version to an unfamiliar yet more accurate rendering. For example, on one occasion, while the Scripture lesson was being read from Jerome's new translation in a service at Oea in North Africa, the congregation reacted most turbulently to an unfamiliar wording in Jonah 4:6, where Jerome had employed the Latin word *hedera*, meaning "ivy," to represent a Hebrew word, previously rendered in the Old Latin by *cucurbita*, "a cucumber vine," or "gourd." Of an irascible temper, Jerome showed little patience with his critics; in a letter to one of his friends he refers to them as "two-legged asses" who identify ignorance with holiness.

For centuries the Latin revision of Jerome competed with the many Old Latin versions. Theologians of the caliber of Augustine and Pelagius recognized the intrinsic merits of the new version, but it was not until the eighth or ninth century that its supremacy was assured.

It was inevitable, however, that just as the older Latin translations came to embody more and more textual corruptions, "being changed by copyists more asleep than awake," as Jerome wrote to Damasus, so the text of Jerome's revision also gradually became altered by scribal inadvertence. At about the middle of the sixth century, a scholarly monk at Vivarium in southern Italy, Cassiodorus, undertook to prepare a correct edition of Jerome's translation. Copies of the Cassiodorian text of Jerome's version were brought to England and Ireland, where the version took on a special form. From Britain, missionaries carried it back to continental Europe (to Gaul, Switzerland, and Germany). In all of these places various forms of the Old Latin translations were still to be found. It happened that not only the usual number of scribal blunders began to disfigure Jerome's work once again, but at each of these places what had been marginal notes of Old Latin renderings came to be incorporated into the Vulgate. Consequently, in the eighth century efforts were made in France to purify the sacred text from these various additions and alterations. Charlemagne, eager to obtain a uniform standard Bible for church use, expressed in simple and intelligible Latin, commissioned a British scholar, Alcuin, who was then abbot of St. Martin at Tours, to prepare an amended edition of the Latin Scriptures. Alcuin, being of Northumbrian parentage, sent to York for manuscripts to help him in the performance of his task.

Simultaneously, Theodulf, a Spanish bishop of Orleans in France, was undertaking a scholarly revision. As a basis for his edition Theodulf understandably used Spanish manuscripts of the Vulgate, but he incorporated into his text readings from other forms of the Latin Scriptures which commended themselves to him as the correct text. Like a modern editor, he entered variant readings into the margin, attaching to each a critical sign to denote its origin. Despite the honest efforts of Theodulf to attain a pure text, the end result of his scholarly labors was to introduce into France hundreds of corrupt readings from Spanish Old Latin texts of the Scriptures.

The subsequent history of the transmission of the Latin text repeats the same familiar story: the usual scribal blunders produced more or less local or national types of text, and when copies of these were carried from place to place, the most bewildering mixture of readings and types of biblical text resulted. In the thirteenth century scholars at the new University of Paris were demanding not only a standard text for quotation but also a Bible more convenient for reference. Various corrections were accumulated and a division of the text into chapters of approximately equal length was introduced by Stephen Langton, who later became Archbishop of Canterbury. (We still follow Langton's chapter divisions today.) Textually the work embodied in this revision was disappointingly mediocre, and Roger Bacon, along with other scholars, censured it as being "for the most part horribly corrupt."

The early printed editions of the Latin Bible were based on the Parisian "corrected" texts. The Council of Trent (1546), having pronounced an anathema against anyone who rejected the old and common (Vulgate) Latin edition as the authentic text, ordered the preparation of an official version of the Latin text. After an inordinate delay, an acceptable revision was finally published by the Vatican press in 1592. This has remained the official Bible of the Roman Church to the present day. Work, however, is currently under way by Benedictine scholars to edit, on the basis of hitherto unused Latin manuscripts, and in accord with refined methods of textual criticism, a still more accurate text of Jerome's Latin Vulgate. Something of the enormous dimensions of the task can be appreciated from what has been said above regarding the mixed and tangled genealogies of the approximately 8,000 manuscripts of the Latin Bible which are known to scholars today.

Early Printed Editions of the Bible

One of the most momentous changes in the manner of producing copies of the Scriptures came at the middle of the fifteenth century with the invention of printing from movable type. No longer was it necessary to write out each word of each copy by hand. Furthermore, printing greatly reduced the possibility that errors would creep into the text. As is well known, the Latin Vulgate was the first form of the Bible to come from the press, being the work of Johann Gutenberg at Mainz about 1456. The first printed Hebrew Old Testament was issued in 1488 by the Soncino press in Lombardy. The Greek New Testament had to wait until the beginning of the sixteenth century to be published. At the beginning of that century Cardinal Ximenes of Complutum (Alcalá, in Spain) began plans for the publication of a sumptuous polyglot edition of the Scriptures. The volumes containing the Old Testament have three columns per page, with the Latin Vulgate in the center flanked on either side by the Hebrew original and by the Greek Septuagint—a position, as the preface puts it, reflecting the central position of Christ on the cross between the two thieves! The volume containing the New Testament has two columns per page, the Greek original and the Latin Vulgate. This volume was the first of the six volume set to be printed. It came from the press in 1514, but had to wait for publication until the completion of the set had received the approval of the Pope in about 1520.

Meanwhile, an enterprising printer named Froben of Basel, Switzerland, had heard of the plans of Ximenes to produce a polyglot Bible. Sensing that the market was ready for an edition of the Greek New Testament, in April of 1515 he secured the help of one of the outstanding humanists of the century, Desiderius Erasmus, to edit such a volume. Working with great haste in order to anticipate the publication of the Complutensian Polyglot, Erasmus used whatever Greek manuscripts happened to be available at the moment. Unfortunately he depended chiefly on two inferior Basel manuscripts, one of the Gospels and one of the Acts and the Epistles, dating from the fourteenth or fifteenth century. Erasmus compared them with two or three others on the same books, but no manuscript was older than the tenth century. For the Book of Revelation he had only one manuscript, dating from the twelfth century, and this was defective on the last leaf, lacking the last six verses. Nothing daunted, Erasmus retranslated these verses from the Latin Vulgate into Greek! This edition, equipped with Erasmus' elegant Latin version which differed in many respects from the Vulgate, came from the press on the first of March, 1516, being the first published edition of the Greek New Testament. Prepared with headlong haste, as Erasmus confessed, and based on late and inferior Greek manuscripts, this edition was altogether unworthy to be the ancestor of the so-called Textus Receptus ("received text") of the Greek New Testament.

Not only in the last six verses of Revelation (where, following Erasmus, the Textus Receptus still embodies several words and readings that have never been found in any Greek manuscript), but here and there elsewhere Erasmus took the liberty of altering the Greek text on the basis of the Latin Vulgate. An example of a totally unwarranted supplementation from the Latin is in the first account of Paul's conversion, where the words of the King James Version, "And he trembling and astonished said, Lord, what wilt thou have me to do?" (Acts 9:6), have no right to appear. They are not found in any known Greek manuscript of this verse, but were inserted by Erasmus into his edition from a somewhat similar phrase in the second account of Paul's conversion (Acts 22:10).

Except for minor corrections here and there in subsequent printings, the basic form of text which Erasmus had edited remained for centuries the only "authentic" Greek text of the New Testament. It was natural that this so-called Textus Receptus became the basis of practically all translations made into modern languages down to the latter part of the nineteenth century.

Important English Versions

The earliest translations of the Bible into English were made from the Latin Vulgate. In Anglo-Saxon times portions of the Psalms and of the Gospels, as well as the Ten Commandments and other passages, were rendered into the vernacular. The first complete translation into English was prepared by John Wyclif and his disciple, John Purvey. It circulated in manuscript copies only, and the complete Wyclif Bible was not printed until 1850. The first English translation of the New Testament from the original Greek was published on the Continent by the English exile, William Tyndale, in 1526. Tyndale also translated portions of the Old Testament from the original Hebrew, but was martyred before he was able to complete the task. Tyndale's characteristically direct and lively style still lives on in subsequent English versions, including the King James Version. The first complete English Bible to be issued from the press was in 1535, the work of Myles Coverdale. The New Testament and much of the Old Testament are practically Tyndale's; only the portion from Jonah to Malachi was translated independently, and for these books Coverdale used several Latin and German Bibles.

The next important revision of the Scriptures in English was published by three Protestant exiles who had taken refuge in Geneva during Queen ("Bloody") Mary's persecution in Britain. One of these scholars, William Whittingham, a brother-in-law of Calvin, prepared the revision of the New Testament, which was issued in 1557. In 1560 the whole Bible was published, the work of Whittingham, Anthony Gilby, and Thomas Sampson.

This Geneva Version, as it was called, was one of the most popular and widely circulated of English translations. About two hundred editions, either of the whole Bible or of the New Testament alone, were printed between 1560 and 1630. It was the Bible used by Shakespeare, by John Bunyan, by the men of Cromwell's army, and it was brought to America by the Pilgrims and other early settlers, many of whom would have nothing to do with the more recently translated King James Version (1611). In the history of English versions, the Geneva Bible is important for at least three reasons: (1) It was the first English Bible which divided the text into verses. (2) It was the first to use the more easily read Roman type (like the type of this book) instead of the time-honored but clumsy appearing black-letter type (Old English or Gothic). (3) It was the first to use italics for those words which the translators added for the sake of English idiom, but which are not in the original.

The scholarship reflected in the Geneva Bible was of the highest caliber. For example, in accord with the evidence of the earlier Greek manuscripts, the title of the Letter to the Hebrews no longer attributed this anonymous epistle to Paul. Among curiosa in the Geneva Bible may be mentioned the occurrence of the word "breeches" in Genesis 3:7, where the King James Version was subsequently to have "aprons"—from which the former is sometimes called the "Breeches Bible." In the running headings at the top of the pages, the expression "a mess of pottage," which many people imagine to be a Scriptural phrase, appears in connection with Esau's selling his birthright. The heading of the passage relating the beheading of John the Baptist is entitled "The Inconvenience of Dancing"! In the margins are numerous anti-Romanist comments.

In 1566 Archbishop Matthew Parker undertook a revision in co-operation with seventeen bishops. A novel feature of this edition was the placing of each translator's initials at the end of his part. Published in 1568 and revised in 1572, it remained the official English version until the publication of the King James Version of 1611. In this Bishops' Bible, as it was called, all comment, in the form of marginal notes, was avoided. Since the several revisers worked without much co-ordination, the style and quality of the rendering vary greatly from book to book.

A Roman Catholic rendering of the New Testament into English was published in 1582 at Reims, France. It was translated from the Latin Vulgate by several English fugitives, chiefly Gregory Martin, a former fellow of St. John's College, Oxford. The Old Testament followed in two volumes at Douai in 1609-1610. The style of the English is characterized by numerous Latinisms; for example, "he exinanited himself" (Phil. 2:7), "supersubstantial bread" (Matt. 6:11), "odible to God" (Rom. 1:30), "concorporate and comparticipant" (Eph. 3:6), and such words as *inquination, potestates, longanimity,* and *correption.* On the other hand, this Reims New Testament also contained many felicitous renderings in clear, idiomatic English, some of which the King James translators of 1611 adopted. The marginal comments are often bitterly anti-Protestant.

At the beginning of the seventeenth century the time seemed ripe for a new Protestant translation of the Bible. Hebrew and Greek scholarship had increased during the previous half-century, and the English language had been enriched by such eminent literary figures as Edmund Spenser, Sir Philip Sidney, Christopher Marlowe, and William Shakespeare. At the suggestion of Dr. John Reynolds, the Puritan President of Corpus Christi College, Oxford, King James I ordered that the work should be begun, and a strong committee of the leading Hebrew and Greek scholars of the day, about fifty in all, was formed. Their instructions were to take the Bishops' Bible as their basis, to consult all earlier versions, especially the Reims New Testament and the Geneva Bible, and to exclude all marginal notes, unless required to explain some Hebrew or Greek word. The work, which began in 1607, took two years and nine months to prepare for the press. The final manuscript, now lost, was bought by Robert Barker, the King's Printer, for £3,500, which included the copyright. It was published in 1611 in large folio volumes, printed in black-letter type, with headings and chapter summaries in Roman type.

The King James Version is the last and best of the English revisions of the Reformation period, and, having embodied the best elements of its predecessors, it finally superseded them in popularity. The rendering was good, clear, dignified, idiomatic, and suited to the people. Though apparently never officially authorized, it came to be called "The Authorized Version." Its merits, however, were not everywhere appreciated at first. Some received it with cold indifference, and others with violent opposition. Many of quite different theological camps raised objections against the theology thought to be reflected in its renderings. Gradually, however, its intrinsic merits came to be acknowledged, and in 1662 the Epistle and Gospel lessons in the Anglican Prayer Book were changed to conform to this translation. (The Psalter of the Prayer Book is still that of Coverdale's text in the Great Bible of 1539.)

During subsequent centuries many changes, some major and some minor, were made in the King James Version. Except for pulpit Bibles, most printings of this version omit the Apocrypha. Furthermore, the current text differs considerably from the first edition of 1611 in punctuation, spelling, and the use of capital letters. Many of these changes were introduced unobtrusively by various editors and printers.

The King James Version served the English-speaking peoples for several centuries, during which the only new translations or revisions were private ones. For example, both John Wesley, the founder of Methodism, and Alexander Campbell, the founder of the Disciples of Christ Church, published revisions of the New Testament (in numerous passages Campbell anticipated the renderings of the Revised Standard Version). In 1833 the famous lexicographer, Noah Webster, published an "amended" form of the King James Version.

During the course of the nineteenth century there came an increasing number of expressions of dissatisfaction with the so-called Authorized Version. Those who advocated a revision pointed to the changes in English usage since 1611, as well as to the acquisition of many New Testament manuscripts far older and better than those which formed the basis of the Textus Receptus. In 1870 the Convocation of Canterbury appointed a committee of revisers, on which non-Anglican scholars were also invited to serve. They were instructed "to introduce as few alterations as possible in the text of the Authorized Version, consistently with faithfulness" and "to limit, as far as possible, the expression of such alterations to the language of the Authorized and earlier English versions."

Soon after the organization of the English Committee an invitation was extended to American scholars to co-operate with them in the work of revision. The agreement was made that the British revisers would give special consideration to all the proposals of the American revisers, and that those of importance which the British should decline to adopt were to be included in an Appendix to the Revision.

In 1881 the Revised Version of the New Testament was published, and in 1885 the Revised Version of the Old Testament appeared. The reception accorded the Revision was quite mixed; the first and prevailing impression was one of disappointment and disapproval, especially in England. The style appeared to be wooden, lacking the vitality of the King James Version. Many felt the force of Charles H. Spurgeon's terse appraisal of the Revised New

Testament: "It is strong in Greek, weak in English." Such a style was the inevitable result of the revisers' policy of using, as far as practicable, the same English word or phrase for the same Hebrew or Greek. In following this procedure for the New Testament about 35,000 departures were made from the King James Version, many of which were felt by the public to be unnecessary and annoying.

On the credit side of the evaluation of the Revision, however, were several undoubted advantages. First of all, the Greek text that formed the basis of the New Testament translation was an older and purer text than the traditional Textus Receptus. Secondly, acknowledged errors of translation were corrected in both Testaments. Thirdly, poetical passages in the Old Testament were printed in lines according to their original structure.

In 1901 the proposals of the American revisers which had failed to win the approval of the British Committee, and which had been printed in the Appendix, were incorporated into the text itself, and the American Revised Version was published. In order to protect the purity of the version against unauthorized changes, the revision was copyrighted, and thereafter called the American Standard Version.

The twentieth century has seen the publication of many Protestant, Roman Catholic, and Jewish translations of the Bible into English. Some of these reflect a particular theological tendency, as does *The New World Translation of the Christian Greek Scriptures* (1950), prepared by the Jehovah's Witnesses, which introduces Unitarian theology into the text and the notes.

Other versions characterized by a distinctive vocabulary and style include *The American Translation* (1935) of J. M. P. Smith, E. J. Goodspeed, and others, and *The Bible in Basic English* (1949), prepared by a committee under the direction of S. H. Hooke.

Several private translations by Roman Catholic scholars have been published, including those by Cuthbert Lattey, S. J.; by Francis A. Spencer, O. P.; and by Msgr. Ronald A. Knox. An edition sponsored by the Episcopal Committee of the Confraternity of Christian Doctrine (Roman Catholic) has begun to appear; in 1952 the volume containing Genesis to Ruth was issued. It is based, not on the Latin Vulgate, but on the original languages, and is being prepared by members of the Catholic Biblical Association of America.

In 1917 the Jewish Publication Society of America issued *The Holy Scriptures According to the Masoretic Text, A New Translation*. It was prepared by a Committee of Jewish scholars with Max L. Margolis as editor in chief. The basic literary affinities of the rendering are with the King James Version.

In 1929, after transfer of copyright, the American Standard Version was copyrighted by the International Council of Religious Education, a body related to forty of the major Protestant denominations of the United States and Canada. That Council appointed an American Standard Bible Committee of scholars from more than twenty seminaries and universities to have charge of the text, and authorized it to undertake further revision if deemed necessary. Such a revision seemed advisable for a number of reasons. (1) Since the production of the Revised Version of 1881 several very old and important Greek manuscripts had been discovered (including the Codex Washingtonianus and the Chester Beatty papyri, mentioned above). (2) Much more information had come to light regarding the meanings of Greek words as used in the common life of the early Christian era. (3) Archaeological discoveries in the Near East had contributed to a fuller understanding of the life and history of the Jewish people. (4) The stilted language of the American Standard Version left much to be desired from a purely literary point of view. The members of the Committee were charged to be no less strict in making an accurate translation than their immediate predecessors had been, but to seek to recover the simplicity, the directness, the literary beauty, and the spiritual power of the King James Version.

The Revised Standard Version of the New Testament was published in 1946, and the complete Bible was issued in 1952. The Old Testament differs from the 1901 American Standard Version by returning to the King James usage of the word "LORD" instead of "Jehovah" and in a somewhat more frequent adoption of variant readings supported by ancient versions (such as the Septuagint, Old Latin, Targums, and the like), as over against the Masoretic Hebrew text. Though some have criticized the Revised Standard Version for what was supposed to be a liberal theology reflected in its translation, its rendering of Titus 2:13 and II Peter 1:1 reflects a higher Christology than does the King James Version. The fact is that it was the diligent aim of the Committee of Revisers to prepare a version that would set forth the Word of God in language that is direct and plain and meaningful to people today. The

Preface to the revision concludes with the sentence: "It is our hope and our earnest prayer that this Revised Standard Version of the Bible may be used by God to speak to men in these momentous times, and to help them to understand and believe and obey His Word."

Conclusion

It is a long trail from the first handwritten copies of the Scriptures in Hebrew and Greek down the centuries to the beautifully printed and handsomely bound editions in our own language today. Probably the most significant change in the format and availability of the Bible came in the fifteenth century with the invention of printing with movable type. Prior to that time part or all of the Scriptures had been translated and published in thirty-three languages; after that date both the number of versions and the number of copies in each version increased astronomically.

Some of the first editions are of special interest. The first Bible to come from the press was the work of Gutenberg (see above). It was issued about 1456 and contained the text of Jerome's Latin Vulgate. The first printed Bible in any modern language was the German Bible of 1466, made by an unknown translator and published at Strassburg by Johann Mentel. The first Bible to be printed in either North or South America was the missionary translation made by John Eliot for Indians living in eastern Massachusetts; the New Testament was published at Cambridge, Massachusetts, in 1661 and the whole Bible in 1663. The first Bible in a European language to be printed in America was Luther's German translation, which was published at Germantown, a suburb of Philadelphia, by an industrious and philanthropic printer and pharmacist named Christoph Saur. In the face of many difficulties and even outright opposition to his plan to print the Scriptures, Saur went ahead doggedly. He collected rags from the neighborhood housewives and turned them over to the paper mill. He made ink from soot scraped from the chimneys of his friends. Because he had only a small amount of metal for type he could print only a limited number of pages at one time, and then had to recast the metal for other pages. Finally, in 1743, he issued the first of several editions of the now famous Saur German Bibles. Bibles in English could not, of course, be printed legally in the Colonies, because the English crown held the copyright of the King James Version, and all copies had to be imported from England. The first Bible in English to be published in America came from the press of Robert Aitken in Philadelphia in 1782. This Bible is of interest because it is the only printing of the Scriptures which the United States Congress recommended for use by the people of the United States.

By the close of the eighteenth century the Bible or portions of it had been printed in seventy-one languages. During the nineteenth century, marked as it was by an unparalleled missionary expansion of the Church, 494 other languages received something of the Bible. By the middle of the twentieth century part or all of the Bible had been translated into more than a thousand tongues. Of these publications the entire Bible has appeared in 191 languages and the New Testament in 246 other languages. The rest have one or more books of the Bible, or in a few instances the equivalent thereof. According to statistics of the American Bible Society, the languages into which Scriptures have now been translated represent about one half of the languages of the world, and are spoken by about ninety per cent of the population of the world. There are, however, at least one thousand other languages into which as yet no part of the Bible has been translated, and which are spoken by a total number of people approximately equal to the population of all of North America.

Besides entirely new missionary translations, many revisions of already existing translations in various languages are currently under way. No translation of the Bible is ever perfect, and several factors contribute to make any and every rendering progressively more out of date. There are three main reasons why revision becomes necessary. First of all, since in every living language the meaning and usage of words change during the years, an older version, no matter how excellent it once was, becomes less and less adequate to convey God's Word to people in terms that they can understand. In other words, though the Scriptures do not change, the languages of earth are constantly changing; therefore revisions will always be needed. Secondly, in another sense the Scriptures *do* change—at least, in the form in which we know them today. As has been explained, the transmission of the Bible by handwritten copies resulted in the multiplication of scribal variants in the manuscripts. The Greek text used, for example, by the King James translators was disfigured by the accumulated scribal errors of many centuries. Making use of older manuscripts which have more recently come to light, scholars today can detect and correct these scribal errors. New versions, therefore, ought to be made from time to time, as more accurate editions of the original Hebrew and Greek texts become available. Thirdly, archaeological discoveries and the study of newly acquired documents, of both a public and a private nature, enable scholars to learn still more precisely the shades of meaning and the nuances of idiom of those forms of Hebrew and Greek which were current during the time that the Scriptures were written. For these reasons, therefore, the Church must never be content with the achievements of previous generations of scholars. Her aim must be to translate the Scriptures into the language of every nation and people and tribe, as well as to revise each translation periodically so as to make it a yet more faithful rendering of the Word of God in the words of man.

HOW TO STUDY THE BIBLE

Any profound or permanent quickening of the life of the Church is rooted in the study of the Bible. The winds of the Spirit always blow in the direction of a rekindled interest in the record of God's saving acts through which the Church was born. It is as natural as breathing for men with a quickened faith to turn to the Scriptures. There they find the story which gives meaning to life now and is the fountain of hope for the life to come. Those who have begun to find the richness of the Bible's resources are eager to increase their skill in study, so that they may hear an ever clearer and fuller word from the God to whom the Bible bears witness. It is the aim of the LAYMAN'S BIBLE COMMENTARY to show how the Bible may yield even richer results for those to whom its treasures have already begun to open.

The aim, however, is broader than this. It is also to kindle interest in those for whom the Bible has no appeal. The Bible is the most widely sold and one of the least known books in the English-speaking world. This is a strange fact—as strange as that every home should purchase a television set but never turn it on, or as the case of the celebrated city filled with shoe factories whose inhabitants never wore shoes. The continued sale of the Bible to people who do not study it seriously may be accounted for in many cases by an inherited reverence for it drawn from devout parents or grandparents. It also may reflect a superstitious feeling that to have a Bible nearby is a charm against danger and a guardian from death. It may, furthermore, indicate that some people have tried to study the Bible, but without adequate guidance have found it hard going, and have reluctantly given it up. It is for such as these that this commentary series is designed, to stimulate interest and offer guidance.

At the opposite extreme are those whose study of the Bible is almost as tragic as neglect. It would perhaps be too much to say that a faulty use of the Bible is as bad as no use at all. It must nevertheless be kept in mind that those who first clamored for Jesus' crucifixion were ardent Bible students, of whom Jesus once said: "You search the scriptures . . . yet you refuse to come to me" (John 5:39-40). It is disastrous to lift Scripture verses from

their context, twist their meaning beyond anything which the original writers would have recognized, place unrelated passages side
by side, arrange verses under topical headings which have no
bearing on the issues of which the biblical writers were thinking,
and make applications to contemporary problems false to the total
thought of the Bible. To offer a better method of study is a further aim of this commentary series.

The purpose of this article is to offer suggestions for studying
the Bible which will stimulate interest, help to correct faulty methods, and assist those who are already digging in the biblical treasures to find richer ore. The article will deal with the proper mood
in which the Bible should be approached, and will present a
method of study which includes the examination of the Bible as
a whole, the study of individual books of the Bible, units within
these books, controlling principles of interpretation, and the study
of specific themes and characters.

The Mood for Study

First, what are the elements of an appropriate mood in which
to approach the Bible? The Bible is a unique book. Although in
one sense it must be read as any other book, there is another sense
in which it cannot be read as any other work. If the Bible were
merely good religious literature, or the record of man's highest
thought about God, the requirements for reading it aright would
not differ from those for other books. It is the faith of the Church,
however, that the Bible is the record of what God has had to say
to man. It is also its faith that what God has here said to man
is said nowhere else. This belief, of course, cannot be proved.
But if it is true, then the Bible is a unique book and must be read
uniquely. If *God* is speaking in it, then it must be read by *listening
for his word* in a mood which is not appropriate for any other
book. How, then, should the Bible be studied?

1. The Bible must be studied *as a book about God, particularly
about God made known in Jesus Christ,* in his living relationship
with men. Unless God is the first concern of our lives or unless
we are willing to have him become so, we shall never understand
the Bible. For all the Bible writers, God was the one central fact
of life, from which all other facts take their meaning. To
understand what they wrote, we must be willing at least to try to
enter into their experience at this point. For many modern men,
God is either unreal or is a conclusion to an argument based on

other realities. For example, it may be argued that since the world exists and is orderly in the coming of the seasons and the courses of the stars, there must have been a God who made it. From this standpoint, however, the basic reality for us is the world, and from that we conclude that there must be a God. This way of reasoning would have been wholly foreign to the writers of the Bible. They moved in the opposite direction. Since God is, there can be a world, they said. The existence of the physical universe was a possibility based on the prior fact of God. The writings of such men can be understood only as we in some measure enter into their way of thinking, and read their works as a testimony to the living God.

For them, God was so far above and beyond men that he can never be known in his essence. Man can never plumb the mystery of God's being. But this mysterious God is living and active, and it is his gracious action in history that can be known. Hence, the Bible is the record of that grace—the record of what God has done for men. Its purpose may be summed up in the words of the prophet Micah: "that you may know the saving acts of the LORD" (Micah 6:5). These saving acts lay in God's gracious dealings with his people Israel, all of them moving toward his final saving act in the gift of his Son, Jesus Christ. The pages of the Bible, therefore, must be searched for their testimony to Christ. The Bible proclaims gospel, "good news" about God in Christ. To understand it, it must be read in that light.

2. If the living God really speaks in the Bible, it should be studied *as God's word to us in our lives now*. The God who spoke long ago speaks today. Hence, the Bible is not to be read merely as a record of God's dealings with his ancient people. It is the instrument through which we listen for his voice to us in our time. Until the Bible becomes the medium through which God speaks personally to us, its study is incomplete. For example, Abraham's willingness to offer to God the best he had—his son (Gen. 22)—cannot be fully understood until it speaks to us about our willingness to offer our best to God.

A recent story about an Indian peasant makes this clear. He had one son. He himself was old. He had striven to give his son an education so that he could support him in his old age. Now the son desired to train for the Christian ministry. This would mean that he could not support the old father. According to custom, if the father refused consent, the lad could not train for the ministry, and would have to undertake his old father's support. While wrestling with this problem, the father heard a sermon on God's demand to Abraham to offer his son Isaac. The word was no longer an ancient word about Abraham. It became a living word to him. The son trained for the ministry!

Or, take the instance of a minister facing physical danger from mob violence aroused by an unpopular stand he had taken. There was no hope for human protection, for the law enforcement officials had abandoned their duty and were even encouraging the mob. With deep fear, the minister turned to the Bible. As he picked it up, the thought came to him with force—the men who wrote this book had no police protection! And as he read the Twenty-third Psalm, the fact of God's shepherding mercy came home to him with a power he had never known before. In both these instances, the ancient word of God became *a living word now*. To read the Bible rightly is to listen for God's voice to us now in the situations we face.

3. The Bible must be studied *in faith*. It is a record of God's action in history which led men to *believe in him*. The record was preserved in order that those who read it may likewise believe. John's statement of purpose could well apply to the entire Bible—"these are written that you may believe" (John 20:31). The Bible is designed to persuade, to lead to decision, to evoke man's "Yes" to what God has done for him in Christ. It cannot, therefore, be rightly read in detachment. If it is to be understood, it requires personal involvement with the God of whom it speaks. As a record of a movement of faith, it can never be understood outside the faith which gave it birth.

To try to study the Bible with pure objectivity, to examine and appraise it disinterestedly from outside the faith, to read it without a sense of kinship with the believing people who march across its pages, is like trying to appreciate the Thames River with no sense of involvement in what it represents. To a visitor who remarked that the Thames was disappointingly small, an Englishman replied: "The Thames, sir, is liquid history!" To grasp what the Thames means to the English, one must enter into the spirit of the long history which has transpired on its banks, and feel a kinship with the people and events and issues which have marked its course through the years. Every patriotic Englishman feels that he was personally involved in all that has taken place there through the centuries. He can say, "I am what I am because they were what they were." No outsider can ever quite be caught up by the meaning of the Thames as are the English. Likewise, no one outside the faith can ever really be gripped by the meaning of the Bible. It can only speak in power when it ceases to be a record of mere past events and becomes the living story out of which *my* faith springs. It is only as the Bible is read as "the sacred writings which are able to instruct . . . for salvation" that its living truth can be grasped (II Tim. 3:15).

But Christian faith is the "gift of God" (Eph. 2:8). To read the Bible in faith, then, is not merely a human achievement. It is wholly dependent on the gracious action of God's Spirit. The Holy Spirit who brought order out of chaos at the creation (Gen. 1:2), who quickened and directed the response of faith in God's people through all the events recorded in the Bible (Isa. 63:11, 14), and who superintended the process by which the Scriptures came into being (II Tim. 3:16), is the one who must quicken the response of faith in us and guide us "into all the truth" (John 16:13).

Luther once remarked, "The inseparable companion of Holy Scripture is the Holy Spirit." Calvin agreed with him, insisting that it "cannot be known without faith" that the Scripture is the Word of God. But since faith is God's gift, Calvin said, "The word will never gain credit in the hearts of men, till it be confirmed by the internal testimony of the Spirit. . . . the same Spirit, who spoke by the mouths of the prophets, should penetrate into our hearts." To understand the Bible, therefore, it must be read with the heart open to the Spirit of God to receive from him the gift of faith, which will quicken our response to this record born of faith.

4. The Bible must be studied *in prayer.* Prayer is the opening of the life to the Spirit of God, so that he may give us the gift of faith. "Ask, and it will be given you" (Luke 11:9) is a law applicable to Bible study. The Bible is the medium of God's self-disclosure to men who by their own searching cannot find him. Since the Bible is the record of this self-giving, it can only be rightly understood as the God of whom it speaks gives himself again and is gratefully received.

Prayer is active receptivity, the summoning of all the powers of mind and heart to receive that which can only be given, the concentrated human effort to grasp that which human effort alone cannot achieve. Great artists in any field discipline themselves, strain after achievement. But when the light finally breaks and they produce some immortal work which all generations rise up and call blessed, they can only say, "It was *given* to me!" It would not have been given without their strenuous effort, but their effort was more the occasion than the cause of their masterpiece. It was the active process of waiting whereby eternal beauty could finally *give* itself to them.

Thus is prayer in relation to God. God does not give himself to the inattentive, the disinterested, the calloused and dissolute. He offers himself to those who actively seek him. Prayer is the active waiting which is necessary to receiving. All study of the Bible, therefore, should be accompanied by a constant outgoing of the soul toward God, reverently seeking and joyfully expecting him to speak to us through his Word. Worthy Bible study is always permeated by the prayer of the Psalmist, "Open my eyes, that I may behold wondrous things out of thy law" (Ps. 119:18).

5. The Bible must be read *in the fellowship of the Church*. It does not belong to individuals in isolation from the Christian community. It is the Church's book. It is the record of a community of faith. It was written by men whose deepest consciousness and most cherished treasure was that they were members of this community. It was preserved by this community of faith through all the generations since it was written. It is addressed to the community of faith. The sense of community among the Old Testament people was so strong that they often referred to themselves by the name of Jacob, or Israel, as though the whole group could be thought of as one person. They were not a mere aggregate of believing individuals. They were rather a "people" living together in covenant relations to God, each finding the meaning of his own life in his relation to the whole nation.

This sense of community, of belonging to a people of faith, carried over into the New Testament Church. The Holy Spirit came on the Church as "they were all *together* in one place" (Acts 2:1). Following Pentecost the Christians were found "attending the temple *together*" (Acts 2:46). When persecuted, they "lifted their voices *together* to God" (Acts 4:24). The continuing mark of their life was that the whole "company of those who believed were of *one heart and soul*" (Acts 4:32). Their faith was deeply personal, but it was not purely individual. Each man believed for himself, but his faith by its very nature made him one with every other believer. Consequently, the Church gathered regularly to hear the Scriptures read and explained, and, in the atmosphere of common worship, to listen for the voice of God in them.

The Bible should be studied personally, but not in individual isolation. Personal study should be accompanied by group study. This means that one's own study should be continually related to the preaching of the Word in the regular worship of the Church. It also means that in Sunday school classes, midweek services, leadership training classes, or special study groups, Christians should seek together to hear the voice of God in the Bible. Through the right use of commentaries and the study of the Church's faith through the centuries, group study may be enlarged to include the Church of all ages. This is important, for although the circumstances to which God's Word must be applied in our time differ from those of former times, yet it is the same God who speaks at all times, and the Word which we must apply to the present will come with greater clarity and force through the fellowship of the saints in all ages. Study personally, but enlarge and supplement and deepen and correct personal study in the "communion of saints."

6. The Bible must be studied *in obedience*. When God's people first entered into a covenant with him, they agreed: "All the words which the LORD has spoken *we will do*" (Exod. 24:3). No other mood than this is proper for true Bible study. This means that the Bible must be approached as an authoritative book; that is, a book whose truth, once it is ascertained, is absolutely binding. It is the only record we have of the faith which centers in Jesus Christ. To be Christian is to share the faith which this book enshrines. To study it aright, then, is to come to it always with a glad acknowledgment that here in this record is the norm by which belief is to be measured and conduct is to be determined.

If this be taken seriously, then the Bible should always be approached on its own terms. It is a book before which we *listen,* a book through which we are addressed. We must never try to predetermine what shall be said to us, nor set any limits within which we shall be confronted. We must not be like Peter on the Mount of Transfiguration, who in the presence of the Lord to whom the Bible witnesses, spoke "not knowing what he said." Rather we must hear the living voice calling to us out of the cloud, "Listen!" (Luke 9:33-35). We should, therefore, come to the Bible not to prove or to disprove anything, nor to make it a tool to further our own interests, nor to confirm our prejudices or establish our preconceived notions. We should not come to it to justify reactionary, conservative, progressive, or radical views. We should not seek to make the Bible an ally of our own thoughts or desires in any realm. We should rather come to listen, to let it speak its word to us, to acknowledge the rightness of that word no matter how hard it may be on us and everything we hold dear, and to obey at whatever cost. The surrender of the will to God is the best avenue to hearing God's word in the Bible.

The result of this will be a disposition to translate what God says in the Bible into obedient action. God is Lord. He speaks that men may obey. Obedience to God's Word enables us to hear him more clearly. Disobedience silences his voice. Jesus' word to the Pharisees, "Walk while you have the light, lest the darkness overtake you" (John 12:35), is sound counsel for all students of the Bible. Light obeyed brings more light. Light rejected brings night. Valid study of the Bible is the kind of listening for the voice of God which shall quicken love to him and to neighbor. And unless that is the mood in which we come to it, our study will be in vain. Said Augustine: "Whoever seems to himself to have understood the divine Scriptures in such a way that he does not build up that double love of God and neighbor, has not yet understood."

It is in this area that the problem of how the Bible relates to ethical decisions must be faced. How is the will of God in specific situations to be found through the Scriptures? To this there is no easy answer, nor is there a fixed pattern which applies equally to any situation or any person. The God who speaks through the Bible is the *living* God, who is free to communicate his Word in whatever way he desires. Certain broad suggestions, however, may here be made. First, a willingness to do God's will in any situation is the most important requisite to discovering it. The truth that "if any man's will is to do his will, he shall know" (John 7:17) is basic here. God may withhold his Word and his will from him who has no serious intention of doing it when he knows it.

Second, ethics must always be rooted in theology. This is another way of saying that our decisions in behavior must always be the expression of what God has told us about himself in his Son. Behavior is not, then, the mere keeping of a set of rules. It is rather the believer's response of gratitude to what God has shown himself to be in his saving activity in Christ. "You have seen what I did . . . Now therefore, if you will obey . . ." (Exod. 19:4-5) are the words by which the Ten Commandments are introduced. The royal law of love in the New Testament is commanded "so that you may be sons of your Father who is in heaven" (Matt. 5:44-

45). The Golden Rule is the expression in human relations of the fact that the Heavenly Father "will . . . give good things to those who ask him" (Matt. 7:11-12).

Third, the best means of finding God's will for behavior is not to wait until some need for decision arises, then with this necessity to go to the Bible for light. To use the Bible as a tool in this fashion may lead to the wrong use of evidence, or to a forcing of the Bible to speak a word which it is not designed to convey. It is better to keep the life rooted in the constant study of the Bible, being a listener continually. In this fashion, the Bible is free to set the problems to which it is the answer, or to point the direction in which solutions are to be sought, without the undue pressure of the necessities of a hurried decision. A constant familiarity with the Bible, bathed in prayer and rooted in obedience, is the best means whereby God may speak his word of direction in any specific moment of decision.

Method of Study

Having dealt with the mood for study, we now turn to the consideration of a method by which this mood may be expressed in worthy intellectual discipline.

The Bible as a Whole

There can be no really satisfying study of the Bible without attention to *the whole story of the Bible*. The Bible is the record of what God has done with and for his people through many generations. It is a long drama, played out on the stage of history, with God as the chief actor and men the minor characters. In order, therefore, to understand any particular scene of the play, it is necessary to know something of the entire story of which it is a part.

For example, to understand the writings of the prophets it is necessary to know something of the role these men played in the history of the people of God. The early period of Israel's history was one of deliverance, forbearance, love. God's grace was written across the history of his people. Events depicted him as a God who was "mighty to save and strong to deliver," who, as Creator and Lord, could use all the forces of nature and history for the good of his people. But privilege involves responsibility. Love involves discipline. Men must also learn God's holiness and justice, and discover that "God's kindness is meant to lead . . . to repent-ance." They must, through the shocks of disappointment and suf-fering, learn that life is not child's play, that the naive self-centered-ness of childhood is folly and mischief. Hence, God's people, nurtured by his love, had to be divided, and each part be increas-ingly harassed by enemies until the national life was gone and the people were again captives in a foreign land.

During the long period of this judgment, the prophets were raised up to announce Israel's doom, to interpret it in the light of her refusal to respond to God's grace made known in the Exodus and in his providential care in the establishment of their nation, and to proclaim that out of the doom there would come a remnant through which God would work his salvation for the whole world. Doom came not because God was either weak or unloving. It was a manifestation both of his love and of his power. The nation had refused to live in right relation to God. He, therefore, destroyed them as a nation. But the destruction was one "overflowing with righteousness," one out of which a remnant would come through whom God could yet achieve his purpose of redemption.

To understand the ethical teachings of the prophets, therefore, the teachings must be set in this framework. They are not mere timeless principles of goodness. They are rather the demands of a gracious God who has wrought deliverance for his people, and ex-pects them to respond to his love with obedience and service. One must know something of the character of the prophets' God and his action in history before their ringing challenge to high living can have its true meaning.

To get some grasp of the whole sweep of the Bible story into which each part is to be fitted, it is necessary to have help. The Bi-ble is large and complex, and the books are not arranged in the or-der of their appearance. To try on one's own to chart the pattern of the Bible as a whole would be too time-consuming, and would de-mand specialized knowledge which most do not have opportunity to acquire. On this account, it is best to get the story of the whole Bible from others who have had opportunity to give special atten-tion to it. It is with this in mind that the introductory volume of the LAYMAN'S BIBLE COMMENTARY has been planned. The article "What Is the Bible?" is designed to indicate the unique qualities of the body of literature which is being studied, and to give some in-sight into its structure as a whole and the best way to approach it. "The History of the People of God" surveys the historical period

of the more than 2000 years with which the Bible deals, depicting
the developments within the life of the people of God themselves
and the pressures from outside nations against which their destiny
was worked out, and indicating the meaning of historic events in
the relation of God to his people. "The Message of the Bible" surveys the progressive self-disclosure of God to his people, as through
the long centuries they learned to interpret the nature of God's
dealings with them and the demands of his Lordship over them,
until at last God's full and final Word was spoken to them in Jesus
Christ. Before beginning a study of any book of the Bible, it would
be well, therefore, to make a careful study of these introductory
articles, in order to have some grasp of the whole story of which
each particular book is a part.

The Study of Bible Books

Although in a real sense the Bible is one book, it is nevertheless
made up of sixty-six different books, each of which has its own
position in the story as a whole, and its own characteristics within
itself. It is necessary, therefore, to try to grasp the individual qualities of each book which make it what it is and help to set forth
its message. Isaiah is not Jeremiah. The Gospel by Matthew presents Jesus in a different framework from that of Mark or Luke.
The Letter to the Romans is quite different from the Letter to the
Hebrews. Each must be studied separately and examined for what
it is in itself, in order rightly to see what place it has in the story
as a whole.

In studying a book of the Bible, it is well to *begin by reading it
without aid from other books*. No interpretive comment by others
can take the place of firsthand reading and re-reading of the work
itself. Even if a book is at first perplexing and confusing, it is better to try one's own powers on it before turning elsewhere for aid.
Full understanding may await help from others, but to possess the
"soul" of a work, the reader must make his own acquaintance
with it. The deeps of a great work must begin to touch the deeps
of our own lives before even the best of comments on the part of
others can be fully profitable. Teachers of secular literature insist
that the best way to master Shakespeare is to read and re-read
him until the creative wonder of his work has gripped us unfor-
gettably. This is equally true of biblical books. They, too, are literature, and yield their treasures at last only to him who reads and
re-reads for himself until he and they have entered into living con-

versation with each other. There is no easy short cut to Bible knowledge. It is only through long and sustained acquaintance, through living with the Bible over the years, that its values may be possessed.

As the study of a particular book is begun, it is well to scan or read hurriedly, looking for the *over-all pattern of the work*. If a man inspects a house to rent or buy, it is quite likely that he will first take a hurried look through all the first-floor rooms, then take a quick turn around the second floor, then the attic, and finally the basement. This is designed to get an initial impression of the house, to capture the "feel" of its general layout. Then, if the house is at all appealing, a more thorough investigation of each room is made. An experience with a book should be somewhat similar. A hurried tour through the whole will begin to reveal its general plan, its major features which give it its own special appeal. In this way, the central drive of the author's thought may be discovered, and even the major divisions into which the work is divided. This should be repeated several times, if necessary, until some sense of the large structure of the book begins to emerge, and the major turning points in the movement of thought are discernible. Although this stage in the process may seem difficult, unaided by outside helps, yet it must be insisted that any serious student of ordinary ability will begin to get a personal acquaintance with a book of the Bible in this way which is hardly possible otherwise.

When this has been done, a second type of approach to the whole work should be undertaken, with a view to making the work *yield up its answers to various things one should know about it for full understanding*. What is the *purpose* for which the book is written? In some cases, this is plainly stated (John 20:30-31; Luke 1:4). In others, it may be discovered by letting the content and tone of the work convey its purpose. The Gospel by Matthew, for example, has no clear statement of purpose. But what alert reader, if he browsed through it looking for marks of its purpose, could fail to notice the frequency with which the Old Testament is quoted, the fact that it begins with a genealogy covering the history of Israel from Abraham, through David and the Captivity, to the Christ, and the frequency of the word "fulfill"? And do not these immediately suggest that the writer intends to present Jesus as the One who has fulfilled the Old Testament hopes? And is this not a clue to why the ones who collected the books of the New

Testament placed Matthew's Gospel first, as the most appropriate bridge from the Old Testament to the New? Once one has discovered the purpose of a work, he can then examine it more intelligently by tracing how the author set about to fulfill this purpose.

One may also ask himself who the *readers* were for whom the work was written. In the case of some of the New Testament letters, this is clearly set forth. In most books of the Bible, however, it is not. But even if there is no clear identification of the readers, there are often subtle hints which at least tell what sort of people they were, what problems they were facing, what their relationship to the writer was. It is impossible to date the Book of Jonah with exactness, or to determine its original readers with precision. But its message makes clear that it was written to Israel at some time when her missionary vision had been blurred and she had no interest in fulfilling the task God had laid upon her that in her all nations should be blessed. The book itself makes the needs of the readers plain, which in turn increases the force of its message.

Furthermore, a work, even an anonymous one, may yield up information about the type of person the *author* was, although it may not name him. To browse through a book as a whole with a view to finding marks of authorship, is an aid to understanding. The Letter to the Hebrews, for example, is anonymous. One of the Early Church Fathers once remarked that only God knows who wrote it. That judgment has remained until today. But, although we can never name the author, it is possible so to capture his spirit from a study of his book that one feels somewhat familiar with him and knows much about him. He may remain nameless, but a nameless friend. He is a man of learning, with a vivid literary style and an ability to reason logically. He is a man of tremendous love for Jesus Christ, to whom he has given himself without reserve and in whose service he lives. He is a man of deep regard for those to whom he writes, trying with all the power at his command to rescue them from the dreadful fate of turning their backs upon Jesus. He is a man of passionate feeling, who, after he sets the stage in argument, can flare forth with appeals to the emotions which would carry the reader almost against his will if he were inclined to resist. He is a man of deep religious insight, who has penetrated to the depths of the meaning of Christ. He finds his readers facing a severe test of their faith, and throws himself with abandon into the task of warning, heartening, pleading, to fulfill his obligations to them as a pastor and to fortify them against ruin. All this, and more, the book itself tells us about the author without naming him. To enter into his spirit as it breathes through his work is an aid to understanding what he wrote.

Another thing which should be inquired after in a general reading of a book is the *type, or types, of literature* that it embodies. Is it simple prose, or poetry, or drama, or apocalyptic writing? (This last type involves the effort to express things about God or the Kingdom of God or the next world which ordinary human speech really cannot say. It sometimes, too, was used as a code language to hide meaning from enemies of the faith in times of persecution.) Does the work embody symbols, figures of speech, parables? Is the work all of one literary type, or does it combine several? If so, can each type be identified? To ask questions like these, and to look for answers in a work itself, is an aid in coming to grips with its message. It has pleased God to utilize all the richness of varied literary types in leaving us the record of his revelation. Right understanding, therefore, involves a recognition of these and the interpretation of them according to their type.

For example, to miss the dramatic element in the Book of Job is to localize and restrict its meaning. This is not merely the experience of one man, it is humanity's protest against the unsatisfying answers commonly given to tragedy, and shows the difference made when we match the mystery of suffering with the greater mystery of God. Or to literalize the poetic word about God "who shut in the sea with doors, when it burst forth from the womb" (Job 38:8) is to ruin it. Or to fail to recognize that Joel's word, "The sun shall be turned to darkness, and the moon to blood" (Joel 2:31), is apocalyptic, is to miss Peter's meaning when in his Pentecost sermon he claims that this prophecy had been fulfilled in the coming of the Holy Spirit.

Much can be learned about a book, too, by a careful observation of *how its author proportions the materials he uses*. If *time* is involved in his work, how much total time does it cover? How much space is given proportionately to any particular period or periods of time within the whole? A recognition of this will frequently give an insight into the author's point of view, and what it is he is really trying to convey in his work. In this way, it is possible to view his work through his eyes.

For example, the Book of Genesis covers a minimum of two thousand years, and if the estimate of geologists is correct, probably several million. An examination of its structure, however, reveals that there is a measurable change of pace just at the end of chapter 11 and the beginning of chapter 12. The first eleven chapters cover centuries or millenniums. The last thirty-nine chapters cover only a little over two hundred years. If eleven chapters cover thousands of years, and thirty-nine chapters cover only a little over two hundred years, it is plain that the early chapters exist as an introduction to the rest of the book, and really to the whole Bible. They pose the problem of the human dilemma to which the story recorded in the rest of the Bible is God's answer. To deal with them rightly, therefore, is not to ask them to yield up answers to our curiosity about the scientific beginnings of the world or where Cain got his wife. It is rather to ask: How do they form the setting and pose the necessity for the story of God's saving action recorded in the Bible?

The same interesting results come from a recognition of an author's proportion of space with regard to *characters*. How many characters are introduced? Where do they enter the story, and where leave? How much space proportionately is given to each? What is the relation of each to the whole work? Genesis may serve again as an illustration. Genesis 1-11 deals with the whole human race. Just where the sweep of time slows up, at the end of chapter 11, there is also a marked narrowing of attention to one individual —Abraham, who was to become the father of Israel, out of which came the Church. From there on, only four major characters are introduced, all members of the same family. Again, the first eleven chapters exist to introduce the main story. God made two starts with humanity in Adam and Noah, both full of promise. In each instance, however, a quick downward turn is noticeable, completely shattering the promise of good with which the story began. This suggests that there is some fatal twist so deeply imbedded in human nature that it is universal and is self-destructive. Is there any solution to this? Only in God. He purposes to do something to rescue man from his sorry plight. Abraham is called to be the father of a movement through which God may rescue man from his plight. He is called that in him "all nations" should be redeemed.

As the Book of Genesis begins with the human race and its problems, it points forward to the whole human race delivered from its problems. But the deliverance is to come through the movement begun with the call of Abraham. It is this call, and what developed from it, that is the center of the Book of Genesis. To recognize the comparative stress the author places on the characters in the book, then, is to begin to enter into the purpose for which it was written. Again, it is seen that the function of the first eleven chapters is to introduce the story of faith and redemption in Abraham, which story is finally climaxed in Jesus Christ, who is God's offer of salvation to the whole of mankind. Sadly enough, the interest of many people lies more largely in questions stimulated by curiosity about these early chapters than in their real function in the unfolding story of the book. For that reason many never come to grips with what Genesis is really designed to convey.

Another feature of a whole book is its use of *places*. Where is the action depicted? And with what significance? Is it important, for instance, to observe that in the Gospels almost one-fourth of the entire story is given over to what happened in Jerusalem at the close of Jesus' life? And is it not significant that Luke introduces Jerusalem into his story long before Jesus gets there? (9:51). By this device the Gospel writers intended to suggest that Jesus' death and resurrection were what gave meaning to all else that he did and said. No miracle, no parable, no pointed saying, is to be understood apart from the fact that it was spoken by One who was through all his life on the way to a cross.

Or, to take another example, without regard to place what can be made out of a saying like this: "O my people, remember . . . what happened from Shittim to Gilgal"? (Micah 6:5). A concordance lists under these names the passages which throw light on the prophet's meaning here. Shittim was the last place where the Israelites encamped before crossing the Jordan (Joshua 3:1), while Gilgal was the first encampment in the Promised Land (Joshua 4:19). These place names, therefore, recall God's gracious act in enabling them to cross the Jordan River and establish themselves in the Holy Land, and the remembrance of this is the basis for Micah's appeal in this passage.

Events, too, call for special attention. The Christian religion, unlike most religions, is a historical religion. It has found a revelation of God in certain important happenings, where the character and will of the Almighty were made clear. For this reason, Christianity can never be understood only as a set of religious ideas. Special attention must be given to the great events in the history of God's people recorded in the Bible. In fact, it may well be said that the whole Bible is a rehearsal of these events—the history of

Israel in the Old Testament and the history of Jesus Christ and his Church in the New Testament—and the interpretation of these events by the prophets and Apostles.

Take, for example, the centrality of the event of the Exodus in the Old Testament. In the book by that name, everything prior to this great event (recorded in Exod. 12-15), and everything following it, is related to it. The Law set forth in chapters 19-23 and the provisions for worship recorded in chapters 25-31, 35-40, are not to be understood in isolation from the central event of the book. These rather are saying: This is the way you are to live and this is the way you are to worship, *because God has redeemed you at the Exodus!* The same is true of the Covenant made in chapter 24. It was made because God had redeemed them. And the false worship depicted in chapters 32-34 is reprehensible purely because it is a turning away from the God who had graciously acted in behalf of his people at the Exodus. To understand something of the tremendous force of this event in Israel's life, it would be necessary to trace the references to the Exodus through the prophets, Psalms, and other writings of the Old Testament, then to study the relation of the Exodus to the new and greater Exodus accomplished by Jesus.

It is illuminating, also, to trace leading *ideas* as they are unfolded in a whole book of the Bible. These never stand by themselves, unrelated to the events of Bible history. They are rather the making plain of all that is involved in history—they are interpretation of events. For instance, in the Fourth Gospel the idea of belief is one of its distinguishing marks. It is never thought of as mere belief, mere faith in faith. It is always faith in Jesus Christ. It is well, therefore, to notice how belief is central in the purpose for which this Gospel was written (see John 20:30-31). An examination of the word "believe" in a concordance, too, will indicate how the idea is worked into the structure of the entire Gospel. One may then begin to explore the use of the word in all the specific passages in which it occurs. Other important words associated with "believe" help to define what sort of activity faith is. One may then look for the bases of unbelief, the reasons for unbelief, the author's analysis of why some people believe and some do not.

By the careful scrutiny of a work as a whole, with the elements in mind which have just been mentioned, the student begins to find his way into the structure of the book, the major turning points around which an author's thought gathers, the leading truths which the work enshrines, and the peculiar qualities or characteristics which set each book off with a touch of distinctiveness.

The Study of Units

This done, the next stage is to *make a careful study of the parts of the work* which have been discovered while looking at it as a whole. The initial inspection of the house is followed by a careful investigation of each room. What is its size? How many windows are there, and how are they located? Is the room well lighted or dark? Are its shape and dimensions such as to make the arrangement of the furniture both efficient and attractive? What of closet space? How accessible is it to the work area of the house? Such detailed examination naturally follows a look at the whole house. So is it with a book of the Bible. After an examination of it in the large, the next stage is to study each part of the work into which the whole is divided.

In doing this, the first step should be to observe carefully the *content* of the section. What units of material make it up? Then, how is each unit of material related to the others, and what does each contribute to the whole section? It may be that in many instances the separate items of which a unit is composed may seem to be unrelated. If so, look for some element common to each item which may be a clue to something which binds them all into a unity. For example, many seemingly unrelated things are told in the Book of Genesis in the section on Joseph. It is revealing, however, to trace through the references to God in the various stories to see how the action of God binds the whole together. This suggests that it is really not a story about Joseph, but about God and his providential working in history.

Or, in Luke 2:41—4:30, the materials introduced seem at first sight to be quite unrelated: the story of a twelve-year-old, the preaching of a fiery prophet climaxing in the baptism of Jesus, a family tree, an inner moral struggle of Jesus, and his experience of preaching in his home-town synagogue. The section begins to take shape, however, when it is observed that the thing common to each item of content is the Sonship of Jesus. And this is introduced not casually, but at crucial points. Within the welter of seeming unrelatedness, therefore, Jesus' Sonship holds all the materials together. Furthermore, to examine carefully how Jesus' Sonship is combined with his role as Servant through the voice which came to him at the Baptism (Luke 3:22), the latter half of which is drawn from the Suffering Servant passage in Isaiah 42, is to understand that all the materials have some bearing on the mission of Jesus as Suffering Servant. This leads naturally to an examination of the rest of Luke's Gospel to see where the thought of suffering is introduced at other places, and how it relates to the climax of the whole story in the Cross.

Thus, to recognize a subtle feature which binds seemingly unrelated materials within one section into a unity, is to begin a study which leads out through the entire Gospel. To be able to see how things within a section are related, and how the entire section is related to the whole book of which it is a part, is to begin to enter into the treasures which the Bible holds for those who are willing to seek for them.

After the examination of the whole, and a study of the major sections in their relation to the whole, then is the time for careful and detailed *study of individual units of material.* This involves coming to grips with the meaning of *words* and *phrases,* trying to determine in each case their exact meaning to the author who wrote them. Unless care is taken to define words as they were originally used, it is impossible to understand a writer's meaning. There are at least three ways to discover the meaning of words. The *use of a concordance,* through which the student may discover every place in the Bible where a particular word occurs, is one of the best ways to find out what words mean. If the meaning is obscure in one place, it may be clear in another. To examine several passages where a word is used, therefore, may help in determining its precise meaning in the passage being studied.

For example, when one reads, "Blessed are the meek" (Matt. 5:5), the question immediately arises: What does the word "meek" mean? A glance at a concordance indicates that the first time the word is introduced into the Bible is perhaps the best place to help define it. "Now the man Moses was very meek" (Num. 12:3). Look, now, at the story in which this occurs. Miriam and Aaron have challenged Moses' leadership. God has judged them for this. But Moses, instead of being jealous of his position and taking the revenge which he, as the leader of the nation, might have taken, prays that God's judgment may be lifted from them. What is meekness here? It is certainly not weakness. It is rather power under control. It is the trustful disposition which leaves issues in the hands of God, and neither goes to pieces nor retaliates in the undeserved rebuffs of life. Add to this another passage suggested by

a concordance, where James contrasts meekness with "bitter jeal-
ousy and selfish ambition" (James 3:13-14), and still another
where Paul reminds us of "the meekness and gentleness of Christ"
(II Cor. 10:1), and the meaning of the word "meekness" begins
to take shape.

A second way to discover word meanings is to *compare different
translations of the Bible,* in order to see what different slants the
various translators give to the word. The Revised Standard Version of II Corinthians 5:14, "For the love of Christ controls us,"
is translated by J. B. Phillips, "The very spring of our actions is
the love of Christ." In Galatians 2:2, where the Revised Standard
Version says, "those who were of repute," Moffatt says, "the authorities," and J. B. Phillips puts it, "the Church leaders." These
help to make clear what the meaning of "repute" is. A comparison
of many translations such as those by Goodspeed, Weymouth,
Montgomery, Williams, Knox (Roman Catholic)—in addition to
those just mentioned—is always a most interesting and often a
most fruitful exercise.

A third way to seek for the meaning of words is to *consult a
good Bible dictionary, or theological word book, or commentary.*
(Specific reference to some of these is made in the bibliography
at the end of this volume.)

Words, however, do not stand alone. They are combined with
other words. It is imperative, therefore, after determining as best
one can the precise meaning of the significant words of a passage,
to study them *in relation to other words to which they are joined,*
by noting *phrases, clauses, and sentences.* If a sentence is complex
and difficult, it is well to try to reduce it to its lowest possible form
—its subject and main verb. This gives the central idea of the sentence. Then the various parts of the sentence should be related to
this central assertion to see what each adds to the whole. In this
way, the mind of the reader begins to gear into the mind of the
writer.

Having done this in each significant sentence, then it is necessary to roam backwards and forwards from the sentence into the
surrounding materials, so that it can be seen where each sentence
fits into the larger sweep of the writer's thought. In other words,
the context of any sentence should control the interpretation of it.
How far back or how far forward one must go to be sure he has
set any particular verse properly in its context will vary with the
passage under consideration. Usually, the total paragraph of which

the verse is a part is sufficient. Frequently, one must go further afield. In any case, for right understanding this process must not be neglected.

Let us take Philippians 3:7 as an example. It is put in quite simple, plain language, which would seem to carry its meaning in itself, and to require no search through the context to refine it. Yet in this simple sentence, if the context is neglected, the reader may miss entirely what Paul means. "But whatever gain I had, I counted as loss for the sake of Christ," he writes. One would naturally think of the things that most men count gain. Does one desire wealth? He must count that as loss for Christ. Or pleasure? Or position? Or power? These must all be sacrificed for Christ's sake. This may all be true, but it is not what Paul is speaking of here. To discover what he counted gain, we must go back at least to verse 4, where he begins to list his former status as a Jew under the Law. Then, a forward look to verses 8 and 9 is necessary, where Paul shows what it is for which he gave up all former "gain." It was neither wealth, nor pleasure, nor social status, nor power which he "counted as loss for the sake of Christ." It was rather his legalistic attempts at saving himself, his own drastic efforts to achieve status with God by good works. This meant more to Paul than wealth or pleasure or power. Yet he abandoned all "righteousness of his own" in order that he might gain "the righteousness from God that depends on faith." The context controls the meaning.

One further aid to understanding specific passages is to watch carefully in the New Testament for any quotations or allusions to the Old Testament, in order to see what light they may throw on the New Testament passage. It is also well, in studying the Old Testament, to try to see how many things there presented are related to their fulfillment in the New Testament. When, for example, Luke tells us that Jesus was dedicated to God through the sacrifice of "a pair of turtledoves, or two young pigeons" (2:24), he is referring to Leviticus 12. There we are told that the normal sacrifice in dedicating a son was a lamb. But if the mother "cannot afford a lamb, then she shall take two turtledoves or two young pigeons" (Lev. 12:8). To examine this passage is to learn something of the poverty of Jesus' parents, of which Luke does not speak openly but which is nonetheless eloquently told by this Old Testament reference. On the other hand, to notice that Zechariah 9:9 is quoted to explain the Triumphal Entry (Matt. 21:5), is to see an element of continuity between the two Testaments which indicates that God's action in Christ was the climax of a purpose which runs throughout the Bible. These interrelations between the two Testaments are conveniently pointed out by the editors of the Revised Standard Version, who have placed references to other passages in the footnotes.

Guides for Interpretation

But when all this has been done, and the student feels that he has a clear grasp of what the words involve, there remains the task of putting the fruits of study together into an orderly and comprehensive interpretation of the passage, and an application of it to life now. There is not much that can be said which can finally answer the problems involved in this. Sheer common sense, checked against the wisdom of the Church through the centuries, is perhaps the safest guide. To illustrate the necessity of careful interpretation of a passage where the words are not difficult and where the meaning seems quite plain, let us look at the dispute between Peter and Paul at Antioch (Gal. 2:11-21). Here is recorded a public dispute between the two great Apostles over a theological question, and the tone of the record suggests that the dispute was vigorous. The facts are clear. But what do they mean? Should two great Apostles have a public difference over the faith? Would these two devout and dedicated servants of Christ, both of whom probably later sealed their faith by martyrdom, have engaged in an unseemly public dispute? In order to avoid the implications of this, some of the Early Church Fathers held that there was actually no real disagreement between them, but that they merely *staged* the dispute, in order to give dramatic proof to the Gentile Christians that Paul's doctrine of freedom from the Law was valid. Most interpreters, however, give the incident its more natural force, which is probably the true interpretation. Here is an instance where the facts are simple, but where the final interpretation of the facts can make a tremendous difference.

A few simple guides for interpretation may be suggested here. Once more, the importance of *the context of any passage, or the various contexts* in which any particular idea is introduced, should be stressed. Had the Church Fathers, in interpreting the passage cited above, taken the context into consideration rather than their own theological preconceptions, it is likely that they would have permitted the passage to have its more natural meaning. Or take, for example, the conception of election in the Bible. There have been many who have understood this doctrine as a guarantee of salvation for some and an inescapable destiny of damnation for others. If, however, a careful study is made of the various contexts into which this idea is introduced, there is much to foil such a judgment. Election in the Bible is constantly associated with the Fatherhood of God. The God who elects is the One made known to us as the God and Father of our Lord Jesus Christ. Almost invariably, when election is mentioned in the Scriptures, the thought of the Fatherhood of God or of God's loving care is to be found within a very few verses (see, for example, Deut. 7:6-8; Hosea 11:1; Eph. 1:3-5; Rom. 8:28-39; I Peter 1:2). God's action and his character are never separated. One can trust whatever "electing" is done by him whose glory has been revealed to us in the face of Jesus Christ.

Then, too, election throughout the Bible is consistently related to service. God's ancient people were called "Israel, my servant, Jacob, whom I have chosen" (Isa. 41:8). Here election is to service. To be elected is to be chosen by God to share in his redemptive concern for the world. It is to be elected to mission, not merely to privilege. And that mission is costly. It involves suffering. For anyone, therefore, to interpret election solely in terms of privilege, especially the privilege of his own salvation, without in his measure taking up his cross and following in the footsteps of the great Suffering Servant, is to miss entirely the meaning of election.

Furthermore, election is not a guarantee of salvation regardless of how one lives. Election is rather to holiness of life. "For I am the LORD who brought you up out of the land of Egypt, to be your God; you shall therefore be holy, for I am holy" (Lev. 11:45). Rather than being of such a nature as to make moral behavior irrelevant, the very purpose of election is conformity to Christ (see Rom. 8:29; Eph. 1:4). To be among the elect is to manifest the family characteristics of the family in which Jesus is the Elder Brother. All of this, and more, will be seen if a careful examination is made of the ideas with which election is associated in the Bible. The context is decisive.

Another important thing is to *distinguish between the Word of God in the Bible, and the mere word of men*. Sometimes even Satan speaks in Scripture (Job 1:6-12; 2:1-6). And Satan will use the words of Scripture for his own ends, if we are not cautious, as witness the temptation of Jesus. But beyond the words of Satan in Scripture and his effort to distort Scripture for his own ends, there are many things recorded in Scripture which convey only the passing mood of men and are not to be considered the message of God. For example, when Elijah prayed that he might die (I Kings 19:4), there is no word of God suggesting that we should do likewise. That was a passing mood of discouragement which God had to rebuke. Nor should we seek a word of God to us in David's dying request that one of his enemies should be slain (I Kings 2:8-9). God's work had to be done in the world through fallible, sinful men, and the Bible records their weaknesses and sins as well as God's message. We must distinguish between them.

A distinction, too, must be made *between the Word of God and the human situation through which it came.* For example, there is a true word of God in the story of the two Hebrew midwives who lied to Pharaoh when he commanded them to kill all the sons born to Hebrew mothers. There is no escaping the fact that when Pharaoh called them to account for their failure to carry out his command, they blatantly lied (Exod. 1:19). Yet, immediately after the record of their falsehood, we are told that "God dealt well with the midwives" (Exod. 1:20). Did God deal well with them because they lied? Could one properly draw from this passage a lesson on the virtue of lying? Hardly. The lying was merely a part of the human situation which accompanied the word of the Lord in this instance. The approval of God was on these midwives not because they lied, but because they so "feared God" (Exod. 1:17, 21) that they were willing courageously to run all the risks involved in defying the word of an absolute monarch. They feared God more than man, and served God's purposes more than man's decrees. That they lied in so doing is an accompanying factor, not to be imitated.

A further distinction to be kept in mind is the distinction *between the form in which a promise of God is made and that in which it is fulfilled.* There are times when the only way a promise of God can really be fulfilled is by a change from the form in which it was made. Many years ago, a father made a promise to his son that if he would maintain certain patterns of behavior until he was 21 years of age, he would give him a horse and buggy. Years went by, and the son made good on his end of the bargain. The time for the fulfillment of the promise was at hand. In the meantime, however, automobiles had come in. The last thing on earth that the young man wanted was a horse and buggy! Hence, the only way the father could really fulfill his promise was to give his son, not a horse and buggy, but a car. Had the father insisted on fulfilling the promise in the form in which it was made, it would have been no real fulfillment. It would not have achieved the purpose he had in mind when he made it. True fulfillment meant a change of form.

So it is with God's promises. The prophets spoke God's promises in a form adapted to the days in which they lived. When, however, the promises were fulfilled in Jesus Christ, the form was radically altered. Tragically, the bulk of the Jews were so tied to the form that they lost the meaning, and could not see that Jesus was the true fulfillment of God's promises, in another and better form than that in which they had been made. The disciples, however, penetrated the form to the meaning, so that at Pentecost, which was no literal fulfillment of the outward aspects of Joel's prophecy (Joel 2:28-32), Peter could say: "This is what was spoken by the prophet Joel" (Acts 2:16). Fulfillment it was, but at a deeper and more meaningful level than a literal fulfillment could ever have produced.

It is well to remember, too, that *not all of the Bible is on the same level,* that there is progress in the Scriptures in God's revelation of himself to men, and that the whole of the Bible is to be interpreted in the light of Jesus Christ. Just as the education of a child is a long, slow process, so God's education of his people took centuries. And just as there are many things which a mature person looks back on in his childhood with either amusement or regret, so there are some things in the Bible which, although appropriate at the stage of Israel's development at which they took place, would be out of place now in the light of Christ. Since Christ fulfilled the Old Testament (filled it full of meaning), it would be untrue to the Bible itself to base behavior on pre-Christian passages rather than on the Word of him who understood those passages at a deeper level.

The Study of Themes

In addition to the study of whole books of the Bible, and of individual units in their relation to the books, a fruitful type of study is to trace great themes. These may be traced through one Bible book, or through the whole of Scripture. Great care must be taken at this point that the student does not fall into the pitfalls noted earlier, where he may artificially join unrelated passages and end up with something quite wide of the mark. If, however, he is careful to set the recurring theme in its true setting in each place where it occurs, and to guard with caution and common sense the conclusions he draws from his survey, great good can come from tracing the development of various themes.

For this process, again, a concordance is useful. By its judicious use, one may discover the relative frequency of the occurrence of any key word, may see in what areas of a particular book or of the whole Bible there is a concentration of attention on it, and may locate the crucial passages to which special attention must be given to understand it. Then, careful attention must be given to the materials which are related to the theme being studied, in order to determine what part it played in the author's thinking, and to help to ascertain its precise meaning.

Take, for example, an idea mentioned earlier—"believe" in the Fourth Gospel. A look at a concordance reveals the rather striking fact that although the avowed purpose of the book is that the reader "may believe" (John 20:31), the noun "faith" is not once used in the Fourth Gospel. It is equally startling to discover that the verb "believe" is used upwards of 100 times—a concentration of use equalled nowhere else in the New Testament. This immediately indicates two things. First, this word is central for understanding both the purpose and the message of the Fourth Gospel. Second, the exclusive use of the verb suggests that to the writer faith is an activity, not merely an idea. It is not only the acceptance of certain truths, but the response of the whole life in an active relation to God. And this response is emphasized not as a mere once-for-all event, never to be repeated, but rather as a continuous process of believing to the end of the way.

But what sort of activity is belief? What are the bases on which one believes? What is the result of belief in a believer's life? Such questions as these are to be answered by careful study into the thought relationships surrounding the successive uses of the word "believe." Moreover, helpful light is to be thrown on the distinctive meaning of belief in the Fourth Gospel by examining the reactions of those who refused to believe. In an abundance of passages where a concordance lists instances of belief, there are unfavorable reactions on the part of Jesus' enemies. Why did they not believe? What was the nature of their unbelief? What is its result? To such questions as these the inquiring mind may find its own answers.

The Study of Characters

Another fruitful approach to the Bible is to study its outstanding characters. The student may take such a character as Abraham, for example, and try to find out all he can about him as he is initially presented in the Bible story in Genesis 12-25. But with the aid of a concordance, Abraham and his significance to his people may be followed through by noting the various periods and situations in their history where he emerges in the memory of the nation. This may even be traced clear through to the New Testament, where both Paul and the writer of the Letter to the Hebrews make use of Abraham to reinforce their thought.

If such study is undertaken, however, two things must be kept in mind. First, one must avoid reading into the story of a biblical character meanings which may be superficially suggested to the mind by a hurried survey, without taking the trouble to check them by thorough study of the Bible's presentation of the character in context. Second, it must always be remembered that a study of biblical characters is really not a study about them, but about *God*. There is perhaps no point at which valid Bible study is thwarted more than here. The Bible is not a record of great heroes who are to be admired, and whose virtues are to be imitated. In the case of Abraham, as with most of the biblical characters, if he is to be imitated, one must choose very carefully what traits to imitate. For the weaknesses and sins of biblical characters are depicted as well as their strengths! The real reason for the inclusion of these characters in the biblical record is to describe God's dealings with them, so that through our reading we ourselves may have dealings with the living God. Furthermore, if they are to be understood aright, the Bible characters must be seen in the light of their place in the whole purpose of God set forth in the Bible. They were all a part of a movement far greater than themselves, through which God intends to "unite all things" in Jesus Christ (Eph. 1:10).

Conclusion

No one method of study is final. Nor do all the aspects of any method apply equally to all areas of the Bible. The ore of Scripture may be mined in different ways. The crucial test of method is the end result, whether the method is able to get the gold from the ore. The suggestions here set forth are elements of *a* method which, it is hoped, may serve to guide some who are searching for the treasures of the Bible. But whatever the method, the final aim of Bible study is to know "Christ, in whom are hid all the treasures of wisdom and knowledge" (Col. 2:2-3).

Selected Aids to Study

Reference Works

A Companion to the Bible, edited by J. J. von Allmen. New York: Oxford University Press, 1958.

Nelson's Complete Concordance of the Revised Standard Version, compiled under the supervision of John W. Ellison. New York: Thomas Nelson and Sons, Inc., 1957.

A Theological Word Book of the Bible, edited by Alan Richardson. New York: The Macmillan Company, 1950.

The Westminster Dictionary of the Bible, edited by John D. Davis, revised and rewritten by H. S. Gehman. Philadelphia: The Westminster Press, 1944.

The Westminster Historical Atlas to the Bible, edited by G. Ernest Wright and Floyd V. Filson. Philadelphia: The Westminster Press, revised edition, 1956.

General

Anderson, Bernhard W., *Understanding the Old Testament.* Englewood Cliffs, New Jersey: Prentice-Hall, 1957.

Blair, Edward P., *The Bible and You.* Nashville, Tenn.: Abingdon Press, 1953.

Bright, John, *The History of Israel.* Philadelphia: The Westminster Press, 1959.

Brown, Robert McAfee, *The Bible Speaks to You.* Philadelphia: The Westminster Press, 1955.

Burrows, Millar, *More Light on the Dead Sea Scrolls.* New York: The Viking Press, 1958.

de Dietrich, Suzanne, *The Witnessing Community.* Philadelphia: The Westminster Press, 1958.

Filson, Floyd V., *Which Books Belong in the Bible?* Philadelphia: The Westminster Press, 1957.

Gaster, T. H., *The Dead Sea Scriptures.* Garden City, New York: Doubleday and Company, Inc., 1956.

Hunter, A. M., *Introducing the New Testament.* Philadelphia: The Westminster Press, 1946.

Kee, Howard Clark and Franklin W. Young, *Understanding the New Testament*. Englewood Cliffs, New Jersey: Prentice-Hall, 1957.

Napier, B. Davie, *From Faith to Faith*. New York: Harper & Brothers, 1955.

Price, Ira M., *The Ancestry of Our English Bible*. 3rd revised edition by William A. Irwin and Allen P. Wikgren. New York: Harper & Brothers, 1956.

Richardson, Alan, *Preface to Bible Study*. Philadelphia: The Westminster Press, 1944.

Wright, G. Ernest, *Biblical Archaeology*. Philadelphia: The Westminster Press, 1957.